PRAISE FOR
SUPERCONDUCTORS

'This is how you build and maintain relationships the right way.' **Tyler Wagner, publisher, bestselling author and business relationship expert**

'*Superconductors* is thoughtful, detailed and genuine, just like Derek himself. If you are interested in optimizing your life including how you make money work for you and not against you, this book is for you! Buy the book, read it, do the exercises and you are sure to have a transformational experience!' **Nathalie Savell, wellness entrepreneur**

'*Superconductors* is a great combination of the practical, the theoretical and the narrative. Derek Loudermilk has beautifully pulled together the insights he's gleaned from not only the hundreds of interviews he's done with the Art of Adventure podcast but also applied his life experience as an elite athlete, scientist, coach and entrepreneur into one package. Love it.' **Jono Lineen, award-winning author and Curator at the National Museum of Australia**

'If you want to live a life of adventure and accomplishment, Derek Loudermilk's *Superconductors* is a book you must read.' **Mark Levy, author of *Accidental Genius: Using writing to generate your best ideas, insight, and content***

'This book will help you to get better at developing high-value relationships with people who can help you to grow your career – which are invaluable skills in the new economy.' **John Corcoran, former Clinton White House writer, attorney and co-founder of Rise25, LLC**

'If there is only one book you read as you start your career, it is *Superconductors*.' **Aaron Hurst, founder of the Taproot Foundation and Imperative**

'*Superconductors* is the career guidebook you can turn to again and again. It is your edge to making yourself uniquely valuable in the career marketplace by focusing on acquiring skills that amplify everything you do.' **Jordan Harbinger, host of The Jordan Harbinger Show**

'Along with helping you become a better storyteller, *Superconductors* teaches you the mindset and tools for careers of the future.' **Michael Margolis, CEO, Get Storied and advisor to Facebook, Google and Dalai Lama Fellows**

'Derek Loudermilk's book, *Superconductors,* is a treat to read. Derek is a student of life who shares his learning – from people, from books and from myriad experiences – in a way that is entertaining and instructive. All leaders, current and aspiring, who read this book will come away with inspiration and ideas!' **Tom Hoerr, PhD, former head of New City School, author, education thought leader**

SUPERCONDUCTORS

Revolutionize your career and
make big things happen

DEREK LOUDERMILK

KoganPage

First published in Great Britain and the United States in 2018 by Kogan Page Limited

2nd Floor, 45 Gee Street	c/o Martin P Hill Consulting	4737/23 Ansari Road
London EC1V 3RS	122 W 27th St, 10th Floor	Daryaganj
United Kingdom	New York NY 10001	New Delhi 110002
www.koganpage.com	USA	India

© Derek Loudermilk, 2018

The right of Derek Loudermilk to be identified as the author of this work has been asserted by him in accordance with the Copyright, Designs and Patents Act 1988.

ISBN   978 0 7494 8236 7
E-ISBN   978 0 7494 8237 4

British Library Cataloguing-in-Publication Data

A CIP record for this book is available from the British Library.

Library of Congress Cataloging-in-Publication Data

Names: Loudermilk, Derek, author.
Title: Superconductors : revolutionize your career and make big things happen / Derek Loudermilk.
Description: London ; New York : Kogan Page, 2018.
Identifiers: LCCN 2018017787 (print) | LCCN 2018019789 (ebook) | ISBN 9780749482374 (ebook) | ISBN 9780749482367 (pbk.)
Subjects: LCSH: Career development. | Business networks. | Success in business.
Classification: LCC HF5381 (ebook) | LCC HF5381 .L667 2018 (print) | DDC 650.1–dc23

Typeset by Integra Software Services, Pondicherry
Print production managed by Jellyfish
Printed and bound by CPI Group (UK) Ltd, Croydon CR0 4YY

CONTENTS

ABOUT THE AUTHOR

Derek Loudermilk is a US serial entrepreneur, high performance business coach, and international speaker.

Derek has been traveling the world full time since 2014 to study entrepreneurship and business across diverse cultures. He has traveled to more than 40 countries and lived on four continents. Along the way, he has learned from thousands of entrepreneurs and helped hundreds more to grow their business. In addition to *Superconductors*, his business projects include:

- Founder and host of the Art of Adventure podcast, which covers global entrepreneurship, travel and personal development. His guests include many people featured in *Superconductors* and entrepreneurs and professional adventurers on the cutting edge of their field.

- Founder of AdventureQuest Travel, where he takes entrepreneurs and thought leaders into the wilderness to take their business to the next level.

In his coaching and writing, Derek draws on his background as a former professional cyclist and research scientist – he is interested in processes and strategy that can lead individuals to get the most out of their careers and human potential.

Derek's mission is to help people find fulfillment in their careers, and adventure and excitement in their lives. *Superconductors* is part of his larger work to help maximize each individual's contribution.

ACKNOWLEDGEMENTS

This book has been the result of hundreds of individuals each contributing in large and small ways.

First and foremost, I want to acknowledge my partner Heidi Van Campen who never let me give up on this project and brought me lots of snacks and love.

To my baby son Axel, thanks for providing endless entertainment when my brain was fried, and without whom I probably would have just kept reading books instead of writing one.

I want to thank my parents, Lynn and Gretchen Loudermilk, who invested early in the research phase of this book and encouraged me wholeheartedly just as they have done my whole life.

I want to thank the hundreds of Art of Adventure podcast guests and supporters who taught me the ideas in *Superconductors*, including the idea to write a book.

There are hundreds more people that I am not naming explicitly, but if you gave me any encouragement, support or ideas along the way, please give yourself three cheers and a pat on the back!

And thanks finally to supporters of the *Superconductors* Publishizer campaign who helped kick this book into a reality by pre-ordering one or more copies when the book was just an idea:

Allen Van Campen, Amanda Taylor, Amber Dugger, Amie Chilson, Andy McLean, Aveen Banich, Bo Rydze, Brandi Roberts, Brendan Murphy, Brian Plegge, Cat Crews, Christina Coppolillo, Claudia Eslahpazir, Colleen Hayes, Dale Vaughn, Danny Kalman, David Randall, Donald Kelly, Dr William Madosky, Mark Prendergast at AB Mauri, Eliot Brown, Fabain Dittrich, Garrett Philbin, Geralyn Basinski, Gillian Noero, Gunnar Garfors, Guy Vincent, Jacob Madden, James Kane, Jane Wuebbens, Jason Treu, Jennifer Rhodes, Jennifer Yaeso, Jimmy Courcelles, Joanna Castle, Joe DiBernardo,

John Douglas, John Brown, Kathleen Harris, Katie Titi, Ken Dorn, Kent Caruthers, Kika Tuff, Kyle Ingham, Laura Latimer, Lee Constantine, Lindsey McCoy, Loretta Breuning, Louis Jebb, Lydia Sturgis, Lynn Loudermilk, Marie Deschamps, Mark Witzling, Martin Leitner, Martins Blums, Matt Lambdin, Matt Wegmann, Meg Mills, Michael Lodes, Mona Motwani, Pete Dillon, Ralph Wafer, Rich Thompson, Richie Burke, Roscoe Sopiwnik, Sal Mariano, Sarah Dandashy, Sheryl Montford, Spencer Fulton, Stephanie Burns, Stian SÃrhagen, Susanne Rode, Terril Van Hemert, Tom Richardson, Tom Edwards, Tomislav Perko, Tracey Abbott

Introduction

Every day I meet people in different countries around the world or on the Art of Adventure podcast, and every day people amaze me with what they are able to accomplish. I have seen people go from losing the business they founded to rebounding and having an even more impactful business in a matter of weeks. I have seen people get fed up with their existing careers and reinvent themselves into a more financially rewarding career that lets them travel full time and have more freedom to work when and where and how they choose. I have seen how people hone their skills and create opportunities for themselves that they would not have imagined just a couple of years ago. I've come to call these people 'Superconductors'. I'm so excited about what is possible for our careers that I wanted to bring you these stories and create a framework for how you can reinvent your own career and explore how you might reach your full career potential.

What is a Superconductor?

A Superconductor is a type of person who connects people and ideas to make big things happen. At times they are conducting groups of people towards a common goal, like an orchestra conductor. At times, they are in charge of organizations, making decisions on large and complex problems, like the conductor of a train. At times they are facilitating the flow of high-powered ideas like an electrical conductor. A Superconductor has the skills, knowledge, confidence and mindset to take advantage of all the tools at their disposal to achieve more in their career than at any other point in history. This book will be your tool to mould yourself into a Superconductor, and use that to create the most epic and meaningful career you can imagine.

Why I wrote *Superconductors*

I have done hundreds of interviews on the Art of Adventure podcast with entrepreneurs, futurists, innovators, artists, educators, scientists, authors, athletes, adventurers and thought leaders. I've observed recurring themes that keep coming up in interviews – noticed the mental models, behaviours and skills that let these high achievers craft amazing careers. Because of my background in science, I like to break things down into bite-sized formulas, which make it easy to understand. This is the book that I wished I had when I was in university, before a decade of trying and failing at different careers.

As I have travelled the world and lived in dozens of countries over the last few years, I have observed the rapid changes that are taking place in how people around the world manage their careers. I experienced people in developing countries such as Vietnam and Croatia having high levels of excitement about being able to craft dream careers for the first time.

To supplement what I learned from hosting the Art of Adventure, I began to dive into the literature around what the future holds for us as a species. Two books in particular – *The Future* by Al Gore and *The Inevitable* by Kevin Kelly – confirmed my sense that we will all be experiencing some pretty rapid change in the global marketplace and that if we don't proactively take control of our career, we will have a hard time catching up.

For example, the number one most common occupation in the United States is truck driving, which previously had safe career outlook partly because you can't outsource driving to someone from another country. However, the first delivery of goods by a self-driving truck was recently made, and millions of drivers are now wondering what their future holds.

We have already seen waves of people lose their jobs to robots and AI. This is a hurdle and an opportunity. All of these workers will have to reinvent themselves to continue with a fulfilling career. On the other hand, if certain careers are no longer an option, it opens up new, potentially more rewarding, career avenues if people are given the right skills and training.

Computers are getting smarter than us in many areas – my calculator is better than me at maths – and are only going to keep improving. But there is hope! Some distinctly human activities will never be replaced by computers, roboticized or outsourced. I learned in grad school that my own eyes and ability to recognize patterns allowed me to identify single point genetic mutations much more accurately than any program could do. *Superconductors* focuses on the most valuable of these distinctly human skills.

What is covered in this book?

The new highest value skills are actually part of our human nature. We are social beings by nature and in our careers, we can draw on our ability to connect, communicate and relate in order to creatively solve our biggest problems. We are also beings that experience joy, enthusiasm and motivation and can get in the zone and be reflective. These natural traits underlie fundamentally different skills to the technical, classroom-taught skills that were valued in the economies of the past. The future economy will reward the high-value skills such as building relationships, continuous learning, creativity and storytelling. Here's a breakdown of what we'll be covering in this book:

- *Career strategy.* To begin, we will look at the elements that make a career meaningful, influential and financially rewarding. You will learn how to combine your skills and talents in a way that maximizes your uniqueness and market value.

- *Foundations.* In this chapter, we will focus on the foundational elements of a powerful mindset, personal energy levels and credibility, which enable and enhance the rest of the skills in Superconductors.

- *Creativity.* Everyone has the potential to be a creative genius. You will learn how to unlock your creativity, get past your internal editor and fear of looking foolish, and some specific tools and exercise to access your best ideas.

- *Doing your best work.* In this chapter you will learn how to choose the most valuable outcomes for a productive career and how to structure your life around achieving those outcomes.

- *Accelerated learning.* Learning is a meta skill that allows you to outpace other people. Learning technical skills quickly means you are more valuable to your team and learning to progress past your plateaus means you can hit higher levels of excellence that others can't touch.

- *Storytelling.* Humans are hardwired to understand the world in stories. Stories can be used to build trust, motivate, persuade, sell and illuminate for your audience.

- *Charisma.* Personal magnetism is a learnable skill that allows you to maximize your influence. Charisma leads others to better recognize and utilize your hard-won skills. We will also explore inner charisma and confidence, which enable you to take more action and create valuable results in your career.

- *Strategic relationships.* All the opportunities you want in your career are tied to specific individuals. Your access to those people gives you access to the opportunities you want. Large and meaningful career challenges often take teams of diverse people – strategic relationships let you assemble the best team for the job.

- *Think big.* A desire to make a change is a major driver of career choice, but many of us are limited by our life experience around how big we let ourselves dream. This chapter will specifically address how to expand your dreams and take action on them.

- *Have fun!* We will explore the power of delight to drive entire industries, and the power of games to improve both our personal engagement in our careers and in an organization's ability to connect with their customers and employees.

How to use this book

Feel free to skip straight to the chapters that interest you the most, or that you think could provide the quickest benefit to your career. The skills and concepts in *Superconductors* are your secret weapon to supplement your existing skills.

When you access the skills in *Superconductors*, you take advantage of something I call 'skill stacking' – where you combine layers of your best skills until you are the only person in the world with your particular combination of skills. And hey presto – you are now extremely rare and valuable in the marketplace.

There are lots of exciting ideas in this book that you can explore in more detail by listening to the full interview with each expert on the Art of Adventure podcast – going back to the original source material to expand your understanding.

The exercises sprinkled throughout the book will take what you are learning and help you start to create real concrete changes in your career. I recommend setting aside specific time on your calendar to work through them. Exercises create a bias towards action, and the best way to truly take advantage of the material in *Superconductors* is to use and practise it.

Think about people in your own life who embody the traits of each chapter – these people can be great sources of inspiration and information for you, and you can model your own behaviours after what you see them doing. For example, when we get to Chapter 7, on charisma, go and observe your most charismatic friends. When we get to storytelling, pay attention to when people are telling a great story.

Superconductors is about giving you a framework for crafting real, sustainable, repeatable career success. It is about getting you the tools, knowledge and actionable resources to take your career vision and turn it into reality. Once you read this book, you will be able to conduct the direction of your career from a place of strength and confidence, knowing you will be able to pick and choose what you want to do, no matter how the world changes around you.

01
Revolutionize your career

When it comes to thinking about your career it pays to look at the big picture. What is the big picture for yourself, and for your chosen field? In this chapter we will look at elements such as autonomy and influence that lead to careers people love. We will explore some of the major traps that people fall into on their career path, such as following someone else's idea of what is good for them or shiny object syndrome, where you chase the latest trends. Because the world of work is changing so fast and we are switching job titles more frequently than ever before, you will learn how to get more comfortable with uncertainty and how to make those transitions with ease. You will also learn how to think about being valuable in the job market by combining your skills and talents in a way that will make you completely unique.

Money and compensation are not the only reasons to pursue a career, but they are important considerations. You will learn how to feel more comfortable getting paid what you are worth, and develop an understanding of how money acts as a measurement for the value you are creating. You will gain knowledge of how to take more control over your career and exert influence on your choices and opportunities. And, finally, you will learn how to maximize the skills and talents you already have, and how to add the skills from this book most effectively.

Connectional intelligence

When I was doing research in graduate school on viruses, the students in my department would meet every Friday for journal club, where we would discuss a recent important scientific paper. The person leading the discussion often picked an article that was of interest to them, and it was usually outside the expertise of our own areas of study. However, this meant we would regularly learn new things that opened up new lines of thinking in our own work. These meetings also helped us become familiar with each other's work, so that when we needed help with specific technical skills, we could call on our colleagues for advice. This was a great system for fostering what I now know as connectional intelligence.

When I interviewed author and speaker Erica Dhawan for the Art of Adventure, she introduced me to the idea of connectional intelligence. She defines connectional intelligence as, 'the ability to combine knowledge, ambition, and human capital, forging connections on a global scale that create unprecedented value and meaning.' I like to understand this as groups of people coming together to solve important global problems. By using connectional intelligence, individuals have the ability to influence more substantial and meaningful outcomes – I like to think of this as pulling a much longer lever.

I loved the idea, and part of what *Superconductors* is about is some of the major pieces of the puzzle of connectional intelligence and how we might use those pieces to guide our own career. Dhawan says this isn't just for the well trained or privileged: 'connectional intelligence is a human skill that can be used by anyone.'

Even in an age where information is ubiquitous, cutting-edge information still is not part of the universal knowledge base. Additionally, there are patents, industry secrets, unpublished research and personal experience. Only when you are able to connect to different communities and forums for information gathering can you truly have the right information at your fingertips. Sometimes the right advice or information can save you years beating down the wrong path in your career or big project.

The Matrix moment

The other day I had a Matrix moment. You know in the movie when Neo opens his eyes after downloading the information straight to his brain and says, 'I know Kung Fu!' I arrived home to find the water to the bathtub could not be turned off. My family had tried calling the plumber but it was late at night and no one seemed to be readily available. We didn't want to have to turn off the water to the house, so the best solution was for me to learn how to turn the water in the bath off. I did a quick search on YouTube and was able to find a video referring to the same model handle. I quickly unscrewed the handle and used pliers to turn off the water. Then I reassembled the handle and it worked perfectly. The whole process took less then five minutes and saved us a couple of hundred dollars. What surprised me most was how quickly I could find the relevant information and put it to use. You can just as easily use YouTube or a quick search online to learn to make a website, send an email newsletter or use the new copy machine.

I had a big realization – everyone will at some point experience an 'I know Kung Fu' moment. They want to know something and then they know it, almost instantaneously. As we approach the point where everyone in the world is able to learn anything instantly, the limiting factor to our use of knowledge is what each of us, as individuals, do with that knowledge once we have it. Had I not immediately tried to fix the faucet, the knowledge I'd gained would have been useless. If I didn't believe the video would work for me or spent extra time doing more research, the running water might have continued. So we must have a bias towards action and get used to implementing the knowledge we have. This book will provide lots of information and exercises to help you along the way, but remember – if you do nothing to take action on what you are learning here and apply it to your own career, then you are the limiting factor, not the quality or access to knowledge.

Career strategy: what leads to a career you love?

There are several things we know about careers that can help us design the right one for ourselves. First, increased skill leads to increased autonomy and more freedom in your work, which leads to more happiness. Let's assume that happiness, fulfilment and compensation for our work are some of the primary motivators in the workforce. Doing work that allows you to use your primary values every day is also important (which is why we do assessments to figure out our values). Choosing a career that will allow you to improve throughout the entire life of the career and continuously be learning means you will never get bored. By cultivating rare and valuable skills and putting yourself in the right market for those skills, you have a better chance of being compensated at a rate that you deserve.

Skill stacking

Traditional education leaves us with a set of specific skills, such as reading, writing, programming, chemistry, etc. Even with a liberal arts-type institution education, everyone graduates with a specific degree or focus. These are what I consider to be the hard or technical skills. These skills are a commodity that fall along a continuum: you can become the best programmer in the world or you can just be average.

But you don't want to be competing on these types of skills because there are people somewhere in the world who are willing to do what you do for less money or work harder than you. So you need to differentiate yourself in another way. Here is where we get to my theory of skill stacking. We want to bring you to a place where you are the only one in the entire world that can do exactly what you do. This book will give you the skills needed to amplify your hard skills, which when stacked make you the most valuable version of yourself.

Here is an example. Say you are a programmer (or a chemist, or an artist – it doesn't really matter). If someone gives you a programming problem you can solve it. You are competent and able to utilize this as a foundational skill. But so are 4,700,000 other people. Let's say you are also good at relationship building, storytelling and creativity. You now have the option of joining a tech start-up doing interesting work that you care about, and participating in different parts of the project that are fulfilling in different ways. You can talk with the media, work with the design team, and explain the project to investors. This leads to much richer and more diverse opportunities than if you are simply good at your foundational skill of programming. Good news: you already possess a combination of skills and talents that make you unique in the world. You are already valuable! This book will help you add a few key skills that are among the highest value-amplifying skills in the market today.

Beware invisible scripts

What voice in your head do you listen to? I interviewed paraglider, rock climber, BASE jumper and wingsuit athlete Jeff Shapiro, who has had many of his friends die from these dangerous pursuits. We were talking about risk management and what voice in your head you should listen to when you are doing a highly dangerous activity and want to minimize the risk of death. It got me thinking about decision-making and why our truth is so hard to listen to.

If it were easy to listen to our true selves, I wouldn't have been divorced just 16 months after I got married. I knew deep down that I didn't want to get married – I wasn't even sure whether I wanted to stay in a relationship. But I also knew that I loved my partner and wanted to make her happy. My intuition was telling me 'Don't get married'. Another voice said, 'It's the right thing to do. You owe it to her after dating for three years.' Yet another voice said, 'Getting married will save the relationship'. Now, with hindsight, I see that my intuition would have been the right voice to listen to.

What about career decisions? What do the voices in our gut tell us?

I followed a dream of becoming a professional cyclist, but then I stopped to follow a different dream of becoming a scientist. This was a very confusing decision because it was a mix of my own dream and dreams that came from other people. Cycling was my dream. Being a scientist was a script I inherited from somewhere – it wasn't totally mine. I always wanted to be an explorer and adventurer, and was chasing a feeling of being a hero. With bike racing, that was covered.

Going after a PhD in microbiology was a mash-up of my true dream of being an explorer (because I was doing extremophile research in Yellowstone National Park) and my invisible script telling me to be a scientist. This invisible script wasn't something I got from anyone in particular, but a presumed destiny I picked up along the way in life. My teachers told me I was good at science and biology, my father was a microbiologist, and I think science is really cool, so all the arrows pointed towards a career in science. When I was out in the field collecting samples, I was living 'my dream', but when I was back in the lab analysing them, I was living someone else's dream. And the rational voice in my head and my intuition couldn't really figure out what wasn't working for me.

I already have dreams for my baby son. I see innate talent and ability in him that I hope he gets to take advantage of. I'm sure many of the things that I do and talk about will become his invisible scripts. Because he is American, he will have all other sorts of dreams charted out for him; his well-meaning teachers and friends will encourage him to pursue one thing or another but he will eventually have to uncover his own dreams beneath all that.

When I lived in Croatia and Hungary, I saw some blatantly obvious scripts playing for people that I directly attributed to these countries being former communist republics. For example, people are not willing to pay to improve themselves. The script says 'learning new skills should be free and provided by the government'. Or maybe, 'I don't believe self-improvement will work for me'.

Here are some more example invisible scripts:

- 'I have to go to graduate school to get a good job.'
- 'Buying a home is a good investment.'
- 'I'll be happy once I have more money.'
- 'If I have kids I need to settle down and stop travelling.'

I love the book *Steal Like an Artist* by Austin Kleon. He talks about modelling your creative work after other people's work that you love, and it will become your own. I've done this so many times in business – started a podcast, crowd-funded this book, become a coach. But you have to make them your own. So how do you tell the difference between what is really good for you (actions that truly match your dreams) vs. another tasty idea that someone else did really successfully but isn't for you?

Pay attention to when you feel discontent, when you feel like something is off, when you avoid doing something or when something is hard every time you do it. This might be your intuition trying to tell you that you are playing a role in an invisible script that isn't for you. Have a debate with your intuition. If your intuition tells you no, play the devil's advocate so you can really understand what the right decision is.

The biggest thing you have ever done

When I interviewed adventure writer Brendan Leonard, we discussed epic outdoor adventures. Because of what he does, Brendan is constantly on the lookout for interesting stories that might make a good magazine piece. And of course, it's not interesting enough to write about something that many other people have done before. 'Family visits the Grand Canyon' isn't exactly headline news. So he is constantly pushed to do things that are bigger and bigger. There is a mountain range in his home state of Colorado that no one had ever traversed. So he called up a friend and they walked the entire mountain range North to South over many days. And that adventure became the biggest challenge he had undertaken. Now all the previous big adventures he had done seem relatively easier. The same thing happens in our careers.

Whenever you hit a new level of career success, you will be dealt a new series of problems. When I went from being a solopreneur to running a multi-person business, I realized that my ability to train my team and communicate effectively were more important than I expected. When you hit another level in your career, all the previous levels will seem relatively easy. Increasing skill, vision and motivation will propel you forwards, but it's up to you to choose how fast you progress.

Power: how to get it

Our careers are not simply decided by merit alone. We are not operating in a vacuum and the influence of other people on our career progression cannot be underestimated. It is foolish to hope that if we are simply good people with some skills, we will rise to the top. We have to work with the reality that we inhabit, which means mastering the social and political ecosystem in our field of choice.

In later chapters we will talk about the importance of mentors and strategic relationships. It is important to know here that within organizations and fields, people in higher, more influential positions than you can greatly influence your career. They can promote you and give you exciting projects that build your expertise, or keep you in a boring, underpaid position. Businesswoman and author Linda Rottenberg told me about the power of 'thinking big but executing small'. The challenge of successful dreamers is to break down big challenges into a series of small wins, with fewer opportunities for advancement.

We are going to need to understand politics, psychology, strategy, emotional intelligence and influence, in order to move through the systems that govern our careers. Even if you are a solopreneur or freelancer, the kind of people that I work with as a coach on a regular basis, you are not operating in a vacuum, but rather can see your career rise and fall along with the people and groups that you associate with. Study the careers of your heroes – who were their key allies? How did they use their power to get what they wanted? In Chapter 8, you will learn how to get connected with people who can positively influence your career and how to ask them for help.

Personal power

Your career is an extension of you and your ability to express your true nature. It is estimated that businesses worldwide lose billions of dollars because of 'covering', the theory described by professor Kenji Yoshino, where people hide their cultural and personal background in the workplace in order to try to be 'normal' or escape negative attention (Yoshino, 2007). Covering can show up when people choose not to engage in conversations, interact with others, or dress a certain way to avoid stereotypes. Erica Dhawan told me about the initiative Yoshino created with consulting firm Deloitte to have leaders to model uncovering by sharing personal stories. This led to increased connection and productivity among people on teams (Smith, 2013). When you uncover yourself, empower the people around you, and you make yourself a more valuable team asset.

Brand strategist, cultural translator and podcaster, Tayo Rockson, is a third culture kid who grew up in many different countries, experiencing many different cultures around the world. The idea of a third culture is that you assimilate your family culture, your friends' culture and the culture of the country or countries you have lived in. Tayo is on a mission for people to be able to leverage their difference. He argues that more diverse teams lead to a broader range of solutions to problems – so consider that you might be the diversity that your team needs. Owning your personal power by uncovering and celebrating your individuality can be valuable for your career – it empowers the people around you, allows you to contribute in more ways, and people will see you as someone who practises courage.

Double down on what's working

Career and business strategist, Jenny Blake, told me that in the middle of her own career changes she spent too much time and energy focusing on what she didn't know, what wasn't working and what she didn't have. She advises that we connect to our underlying strengths and interests that have stayed with us our entire lives. Sometimes I ask new clients: 'What has your whole life prepared you to do? Combine all your experiences from all areas of life. What kind of role or task would bring all the best of what you have learned from life to bear?'

In order to create the career you want going forward, a strong sense of who you are is important. This is a multidimensional understanding: who you are when you strip away your skills, talents, previous experience, etc. My favourite way to learn this is by going on adventures and taking on big challenges. Getting feedback from your peers and colleagues can give you good perspective. Self-assessments such as the strengths finder and Myers–Briggs are popular and helpful as well. Roger Hamilton's wealth dynamics assessment is another one that I have found useful.

'Knowing your purpose pattern and how to act on it is one of the most important drivers in our economy today,' says Aaron Hurst, founder of Imperative. Use self-assessment tools, reflection and feedback to help you identify what brings you a feeling of purpose, and then come up with world-changing goals that align with your pattern.

EXERCISE

Make a list of the self-assessment tools you would like to use, and schedule a time to use them.

The power of the interview

Before I started my career I heard about the informal interview. The guidance counsellor at my college told me to have coffee meetings with people in different fields and ask them for advice. Of course, none of us knew what we were doing and we mostly thought this was just a way to set up asking for a job later on.

When my business coaching clients pick a type of business they want to run, I often have them go out and do a series of interviews with people in their field. This helps us to fully understand the main drivers of success in the chosen field. You will learn more about this deconstruction process in Chapter 5. We also learn from the interviewee about how expectations they had on entering the field matched the reality. We are trying to discover if our understanding of a given field is accurate. When I was in graduate school for microbiology, I learned that my expectation of doing lots of field work didn't match the laboratory and computer-heavy work I ended up doing. I could have learned more about where I would be spending my time, before I started.

Here are some good questions to ask when you are doing your discovery work:

- Who is doing really well in this field that you wouldn't expect?
- Where are people getting rich in this field?

- What types of things are the leaders in your field known for?
- What types of projects have led to the biggest benefits for your career?
- What didn't you expect going into this career?

I took this idea and turned it into the Art of Adventure podcast – I wanted to fully understand what it took to be a professional adventurer. As you know, those interviews eventually led to the creation of this book. What I find over and over again from the many guests on the show who are published authors is that there is always something useful they tell me that never made it into the book.

Avoid shiny object syndrome

As a business coach for entrepreneurs who want to work from anywhere while they travel the world, I naturally attract people who don't want to be tied down. This can manifest itself as people not wanting to be tied to any certain business model and therefore end up jumping ship for the next 'shiny object' or interesting idea that might work for them, even before they finish their last project. This is also a reflection of myself and I force myself to do things like write this book and be a good dad, both of which are long-term, difficult, focus-oriented projects. It is important that we enable ourselves to concentrate our forces on key projects and allow us to maximize the resources we have at our disposal. Knowing that career change is happening more frequently and can exacerbate the situation, it is more important than ever that you start what you finish. Before you try a new career strategy or business strategy, ask yourself if you have mastered the basics in your chosen field. Shiny object syndrome happens when people aren't getting the result they want. If you haven't mastered the core drivers of success in your field, jumping to a new strategy still won't work for you. If you experience shiny object syndrome and are tempted to leave an incomplete project, first check in with why you were doing that project in the first place. If that reason is still important to you, and the results still benefit you, keep going.

Say yes, then no

Early in your career you want to say 'yes' as much as possible. Entrepreneur, Derek Sivers, tells the story of when he was a young musician getting his start. He said yes to every gig that was offered to him, even if he wasn't getting paid or had to haul his instruments all the way across town, because he never knew which one might lead to a big break. It's the same principle that venture capitalists operate under – if a small percentage of the businesses they invest in succeeds, that will more than make up for the majority that fail, which depending on the data you use shows between 60–75 per cent failure rate (Griffith, 2017).

Once you start to experience success, however, you need to start saying no. This is because you will have determined what a productive career looks like for you. If you determine that you are going to be a YouTube star, then you need to be making lots of quality YouTube videos. Opportunities to take a job as an announcer or write books or make podcasts might be appealing, but they will likely come at the expense of your most important output – videos.

What the market wants

When thinking about our careers, it might be useful to consider what the market wants. This is where the money will come from, which is the differentiating factor between a career and a hobby. Money is the proof that you are doing something valuable and is a great metric to use for determining how valuable you are.

In business we say that there must be a product–market fit. Basically, that if you have created a product or service, there needs to be someone willing and able to pay for this product. If instead you are the product, there must be a market willing and able to pay for what you are offering. Some markets reward people much more significantly financially than others. For example, schoolteachers are generally paid much less than doctors. If you have specific financial compensation goals, or want to guarantee continuous employment, it pays to have a good understanding of what your chosen market will bear and how well you match the needs of that market.

As a former microbiologist, I was well acquainted with the academic science job market in the United States. One of the reasons that I left science is because the market would not bear the supply of new scientists. This is because funding has been going down for research science, even as the number of well-trained scientists has been going up. What I see is that highly skilled PhDs are unable to create a career that they love because they are piecing together scraps of a career one or two years at a time at different universities. I have friends that are leaving the United States to work in Canada or the United Kingdom – potentially better markets for their skills. You cannot simply hope that if you are good at what you do, that will bail you out, if the market is not there for your skills.

Talent follows money – a country or organization that decides to compensate certain skills will be able to draw or steal talent from other countries and organizations. This is what drives the high pay rates and bonuses for people like bankers and programmers in the United States, or what allows Manchester United to consistently hire the best football players.

Imagine you are hiring

Let's imagine that you are hiring someone for a position within your organization. You want to have that person bring in at least as much value as they are costing you in salary or payment. Companies have established metrics to know the results they should be expecting from different types of employees. If an employee is costing you more than they bring in, you are likely to let them go.

There are other, more subtle things that you will consider when hiring someone. Will this person fit in with my team? Pro athletes are sometimes brought to new teams for their leadership or clubhouse skills as much as for their physical prowess. Will this person make my life easier or harder? Will they be a pain in the butt? How do they handle new situations and responsibility? As I have hired my own team, I have learned that I really like people who will take action on something without having to come back to me over and over for clarification, because this saves me from hours of unnecessary extra email and communication.

People are hiring because they want specific results. You hire a marketing person to help you reach more people. There are many ways to run a marketing campaign, so the specific skills may be different, but the result will be the same – more people know about the business and therefore there are more customers.

Does this help change the way you think about the value that you bring to the table when someone is hiring you? If you can emulate the qualities you would look for while hiring, it will help your own efforts to have someone hire you. How can you ensure your worth is greater than your salary? How can you guarantee the results you were brought on to achieve? Would you hire yourself?

Your relationship with money

Even if you have a combination of rare and valuable skills, your mental programming and upbringing may have left you with a relationship with money that does not help you with your ideal career. If you know your market value but are unwilling to ask for the salary you deserve, you will resent whoever is paying you because you are working harder than you know you ought to.

An important piece of the career puzzle is your ability to receive compensation for your work. This is where the ego can get in your way – by over-valuing yourself and pricing you out of the market, or by undervaluing yourself because you want to make sure that everyone loves you. Either way, you need to zoom out and make the value exchange less personal. If a person is providing an amazing value for their clients or employer, you would expect them to be well paid, right? That should not change if you are that person. If you believe that rich people are bad, or that money is the root of all evil, those thoughts will undermine your ability to accept more money. Look for examples of wealthy people who are kind, generous, and wise with their money. Money is a tool that allows you to impact your world, create opportunities, and increase your enjoyment of life. If we are going to bother crafting a career to do these things, we also want to have a relationship with money that matches our efforts.

EXERCISE – Embrace financial abundance

To realign your thoughts to be comfortable with financial compensation for your work, consider these questions: How does money reduce my stress? How does money give me freedom? How will I use money for the good of the world once I earn it? How can I be friends with money? Why do I deserve to make money in my career (come up with 100 reasons here)? Who do I need to be to handle making more money?

Ambition

Have you ever seen an athlete or a business person that had great talent defeated by someone with less innate skill but more ambition? Career success is about more than talent – it's our ability to maximize what we have. Ambition is about raising your standard for what you will accept for yourself and what you want to achieve. The difference is when you say, 'I must succeed' vs. 'I really should do that if I want to succeed'. Beware of reducing your ambition just because you don't see all the steps to achieve your goals – it can be tempting to reduce your ambition when you haven't yet acquired the skills or knowledge needed to achieve them. Don't let other people telling you to aim lower change how you show up for your career. Don't be afraid to own that you really care about your career success and your goals.

Accessing networks

I'm part of a mastermind for coaches – there are 30 of us that all pay to be part of this programme. In it, we work on various aspects of our business together – improving sales, our online marketing, giving better talks and presentations, and improving our coaching. We have access to a team of coaches and are paired with a buddy within the group. When one of us has a problem or challenge that arises in our business, we post in our shared Facebook group and the whole community helps solve the problem. I have seen most members of our community grow their business by 200–500 per cent in the last year that we have been working together.

We all have access to information, but what's important is how we use that information in the service of our goals. And having other members, a cohort of peers, working right alongside you allows you to see the result of various different types of people implementing and working on the same types of projects. We send business to each other in the form of clients, and we make introductions to each other to key influencers who can help each other's goals.

There are a few ways you can find a group like this in your own career field. There are often professional organizations in fields that have existed for many years. Remember the graduate school journal club I talked about at the beginning of the chapter? Networks of students like that have existed for centuries. For newer fields (such as crypto currencies and VR), you might need to start your own, especially if you want to meet up with people locally in real life. You can use Meetup.com to start your own event. LinkedIn and Facebook groups are great places to start online. Paid membership will give you access to higher level people – I even know some entrepreneurs who are willing to pay $100,000 per year for membership in exclusive mastermind groups. In Chapter 8 you will learn how to find the most well-connected people who can help bring you into the networks you want to be a part of.

Complementing others

If you picked up this book and thought, 'wow, I need to get good at everything so that I can outcompete everyone and get my choice career', you might be feeling a little stressed. Keep in mind that unless your aim is to be a solopreneur, you will likely not be the only one on your team or organization. You will be part of a unit, a piece of the puzzle for making something happen in the world. So you don't have to be good at everything. You will complement other members of your team. It's very freeing to know that even if you will be working online, you don't have to be a good programmer, or even if you are going to be in the marketing department, you don't have to know Photoshop. You can always find someone to shore up the technical skills you haven't acquired.

Embrace uncertainty

In our interview, career change expert Jenny Blake told me the average position lasts only two years – instead of two decades a generation ago. My own career has changed and evolved many times over the decade that I have been part of the workforce. So plan for a career that evolves. Expect that you will learn new things about yourself and your interests and skills as you try things.

Sometimes, by taking action in our career we encounter unexpected turns that give unexpected benefits. We know that the mission to put a man on the moon by the United States led to all kinds of advances in rocketry and computing technology that jumpstarted the success of the US economy for the last 60 years. Christopher Columbus dreamt of finding an easier route to India and instead opened up exploration of an entirely new continent. When I started the Art of Adventure podcast, I had no idea so many good things would come from it – like this book, speaking opportunities, a coaching practice and the AdventureQuest trips. If you demand certain things from your career, you might suffer disappointment when something different happens. So why not ask to be pleasantly surprised by your career?

The adventure mindset

One of my mentors, Rick Hanson, asked me – what will you be the best in the world at? I decided that I would become the world's leading expert on adventure. To that end I have read hundreds of the greatest adventure books and journals and interviewed the world's greatest adventurers. Your complete guide to being a professional adventurer will have to wait until the next book, but for now it is useful for us to apply the adventure mindset for a career.

The key elements of an adventure are that it must be remarkable, which means you must have a story to tell about it. There must be some risk involved – whether real or perceived risks. That is the root of the etymology of the world venture/adventure – to take a risk. And, finally, the adventurer must undergo some change. Over and over, guests on my podcast tell me the importance of getting comfortable being uncomfortable. Let's look at our careers as an adventure. When we are intentionally challenging ourselves and getting into new situations that make us a little uncomfortable, that opens the possibility of something incredibly exciting to come from that. What if your career could be a bold and exciting adventure?

Think about the great explorers and adventures of the past – they were constantly going where no one had gone before. The modern adventure credo is to do something the fastest, farthest, or first (and ideally all three). Adventurers are the type of people who create something where before there was nothing. Because our world is changing so rapidly, you can either be proactive or reactive and try to catch up. By bringing the adventure mindset to your career you can set your own course rather than becoming obsolete and trying to reinvent yourself out of necessity. In the hero's journey, it's not about the physical treasure the hero brings back from his adventure, it's about who he has become. When we seek to develop a career we love, it's not what we get from our career, it's who we become.

Conclusion: there is only one YOU

Hopefully by now you are feeling pretty good about your career potential – you already have what it takes to have an awesome career. In this chapter we've covered career strategy and the elements that make a career you love. You've learned:

- how to value yourself and how to get the salary you deserve;
- how your combination of skills makes you unique in all the world and ideally prepared to combine those skills for good use;
- how to use interviews to uncover information about your chosen field, and how to say yes to lots of opportunities, while avoiding getting distracted;
- how to zoom out and look at your career from the perspective of the market and potential employers to identify what is valuable; and
- how to embrace uncertainty and treat your career like the exciting adventure it can be.

In the next chapter, you will learn about some of the not-so-obvious foundations that will enable your career success and make all the other skills in this book easier.

Works cited

Griffith, E (2017, 27 June) *Conventional Wisdom Says 90% of Startups Fail. Data Says Otherwise.* Retrieved 22 February 2018, from Fortune: http://fortune.com/2017/06/27/startup-advice-data-failure/

Smith, K Y (2013) *Uncovering Talent: A new model of inclusion*, Deloitte University

Yoshino, K (2007) *Covering: The hidden assault on our civil rights*, Random House, New York

02

Build a strong foundation

Safety first, then get paid, then do your best work.
MY BOSS AT MY FIRST EVER JOB AT 3M

To have the career you want, you need to be a high performer. To be a high performer, you need a certain baseline or foundation for yourself. Did you ever learn about Maslow's hierarchy of needs? Maslow describes five fundamental elements needed in order to reach the stage of self-actualization: physiological needs, safety needs, love and belonging needs, esteem needs and self-actualization needs. Making sure you have the first levels of these needs met is foundational to being able to work on the final levels of esteem and self-actualization.

It's so much easier to create the career you want when you have your health, your relationships are going well, you have some savings in the bank, and you know where your next paycheque is coming from. So let's establish some foundations for our career, which we can build specific rare and valuable skills upon. The three foundational elements in this chapter are mental, energetic and credibility foundations.

Mental foundations

Mindset

When I asked Jenny Blake, author of *The Pivot Method*, what the most important skill for any career was, she said getting your mindset right. In the business coaching world, my fellow coaches and I say that our work is 5 per cent strategy and 95 per cent mindset training. The difference between two world-class athletes winning and losing on a specific day comes largely down to their mindset. Carol Dweck, author of *Mindset*, tells us that operating under a 'growth mindset' instead of a fixed one will enhance our career. Growth mindset is the underlying belief that you can learn and grow and acquire new skills. A fixed mindset is the belief that you are born with certain set levels of innate skills and talents. Growth mindset individuals worry less about looking smart and spend more time learning, which leads to greater career success. The challenge to embody the growth mindset is to overcome our own insecurities about our abilities. Many of the key elements of careers of the future – such as collaborating, innovating, sharing ideas and feedback – are founded in a growth mindset.

Empathy and emotional intelligence

Erica Dhawan told me that strong emotional intelligence is an important building block for connectional intelligence. In his book *Humans Are Underrated*, author Geoff Colvin says that there are certain things that only humans will be able to do for each other (and not robots or AI) (Colvin, 2015). These activities involve empathy and are the basis for what Colvin calls the relationship economy. So how do we build more empathy and thus demand?

In his ground-breaking book, *Emotional Intelligence*, Daniel Goleman defines emotional intelligence (EQ) as your ability to be aware of and regulate to your feelings (Goleman, 1995). Students with higher levels of empathy get better grades because they are better able to manage their emotions. Managers with higher EQ are more persuasive and thus better leaders. Goleman suggests that mirroring other people's posture and body language will help you understand their feelings. We will learn more about how our physical body is tied to and can influence our emotions in Chapter 7.

As the host of the Art of Adventure, I have noticed that adventure can be a major contributor to empathy. Travellers and adventurers are constantly relying on the kindness of others, and experiencing life situations different than their own. You can grow your empathy by spending time with different people at work, seeking new experiences in your community, travelling, and reading about different cultures.

Willpower

I often have my clients take on a big physical challenge at the same time as they are working on their business. Besides helping them become master of their schedule, training for an event like a marathon helps you build willpower. We are cognitive misers – our brains are wired to spend less energy and solve problems in less effortful ways. Because of this, we have a limited amount of willpower and decision-making ability to use each day. There are two ways to improve on this situation: get more willpower and use less of it. So, when you are doing a workout, you must use willpower to keep the effort level high, when your body is burning with pain and telling you to slow down or back off. You are forcing your body to inhabit the state you want rather than the state it wants. You are training your ability to bring considerable willpower to an activity, and then recover from it. We also want to learn to structure our lives to make the best use of our limited decision-making ability, as you will see Barack Obama did as president in Chapter 4.

One of the aims of this book is to help enhance your autonomy by helping you become more valuable. When I talk to people who want to leave the corporate world and become entrepreneurs, one of the first things they tell me is that they don't like doing things for someone else. This is because it burns our willpower up to force ourselves to do something that we don't want to do for someone else. If you are doing work for someone else, make sure you make it your own choice by being informed, rather than blindly following orders.

Understanding habits

Another key piece of our mental foundation involves acquiring beneficial habits. Strong habits are essential to long-term career success (and happiness) because they help us unconsciously and effortlessly repeat desirable behaviours. In the book *The Power of Habit*

(Duhigg, 2012) we learn about the habit loop. Habits start with a cue, which leads to a behaviour, which gives you a reward. For a habit like smoking, for example, the cue might be a reprimand from your boss, your behaviour is smoking, and the reward is a release of that tension. You can change the behaviour within a habit loop if you keep the cue and the reward the same. So you could swap out jumping jacks for smoking a cigarette and have the habit remain intact. Once you understand how habits lead to your behaviours, you can tailor your habits into career advancing behaviours.

Sometimes intention to change a habit and knowledge of habit-forming behaviour isn't enough. When I was first studying charisma, I set a trigger for myself: whenever I walked through a doorway, I made sure to stand up tall, smile, and bring a positive energy. I wanted to help establish the habit, and I knew that people often form their first impression of you when you walk into a room, so I chose the doorway as my trigger. If you decide you want to act a certain way to benefit your career – helpful, joyful, courageous – you can set an alarm on your phone to go off throughout the day to remind you of the traits you are attempting to make a habit. Think of the foundations in this chapter as habits that help you build a successful (and satisfying) career.

Thought patterns

One of my mentors, Rick Hanson, is a neuroscientist who helps people become permanently happier. We all have a genetic set point for happiness, but we can change this through neuroplasticity. Neuroplasticity is when the neurons in the brain form new connections, thoughts and memories over time as we learn. We will take advantage of this biology in Chapter 5. Just as we can learn and change our happiness levels, we can change or programme our mind to work in different ways. If you can get your thought patterns into an optimal state, where you don't hold yourself back and take yourself out of the game, you will overcome one of the major hurdles that holds people back from their dream career. Hanson's advice is to take 20 or more seconds to enjoy experiences that make you happy. You can also use journaling to relive a positive experience from the previous day. To change your thought pattern to a solution-oriented one, instead of asking, 'What are the ways this could go wrong?' you can ask 'How might we make this work?'

Your personality comes from your thoughts, but you are more than your thoughts. Most of your thoughts are the same from day to day, which leads to you having the same experience from day to day. If that experience of your life is disempowering in any way, it will continue to affect you until you change your thoughts.

Negative thoughts can consume you. I have seen alive, passionate and motivated individuals slip into negative thought patterns and enter depression, taking themselves out of the game. Look out for this! How do you keep negative thoughts out? If you have no room for them, if you are completely absorbed in your work, if you find the state of flow, you can keep them out. If you are feeling gratitude, you can keep them out. It is difficult to hold feelings of gratitude and negative thoughts in your mind at the same time.

Start with happiness

In his TEDx talk, Shawn Achor tells us that only 25 per cent of career success is affected by IQ. The remaining 75 per cent is due to your optimism levels, social support, and your ability to see stress as a challenge instead of a threat. Achor says that the formula for success that most people follow is to simply work harder. People base their future happiness on achieving that success. What happens is that once people achieve something they want, they move the goalpost to a new higher measure and they keep pushing their happiness into the future. What Achor encourages is that we make ourselves perform better and have more success by starting with a positive foundation. When you are using positive thinking, you get a surge of dopamine, which besides making you happy, activates all the learning centres of the brain.

EXERCISE – Random act of kindness

Write one email praising or thanking someone in your social network. Shawn Achor found that this one simple act can help you focus on the positive, which can put your brain in a more productive state.

Control the image in your mind

If I tell you 'don't think about ice cream', what happens? You probably came up with a picture of ice cream in your mind. The picture in your mind comes from the things you think, talk, write about and encounter throughout your day.

When you reinforce a positive behaviour (a habit that benefits your career), you increase the likelihood of it happening again. How do you reinforce a behaviour? Talk about it, tell the story of your success, share your wins. Replay it in your mind. Write about it. Tell yourself specifically what part you did well with. Praise other people for their excellent performances.

On the flip side, because of our natural focus on the negative, we often negatively reinforce the images in our mind. We replay our mistakes and beat ourselves up over them. We focus on and point out other people's mistakes. We complain to build connection with others.

Performers of all kinds, from actors to athletes, rehearse their performance. Olympic gold medallist and mental performance trainer Lanny Bassham has created a mental management system to help control your thoughts to change your result. Visualize yourself doing the skill you want to perfection. In your mind, you can do it right every time. This completely avoids any negative focus. Because we are becoming familiar with something through rehearsal, we lose our sense of the unknown and it diminishes our fear (Bassham, 1996).

Get comfortable with yourself as a high achiever. Some people say 'Just my luck' when something bad happens to them. What if you said 'Just my luck' every time something good happened? When you rehearse the image of yourself doing something extraordinary, reinforce that by saying 'I am the kind of person who does something extraordinary'. Then when you get to the real performance, your upper limit won't be triggered.

Understand your thoughts

If we are going to have a strong mental foundation, the first major move is to go from unconscious thought to conscious thought. This means that we are able to observe what we are thinking. This is where mindfulness practice comes in. There will be different meditation practices and mindfulness methods that appear throughout this book. What you need to know is that because your daily routines, experiences, friends and activities are largely the same from day to day, you are creating the same inputs for your brain and you will largely get into thought patterns and habits. These become comfortable routines for us. Even if we don't necessarily like the thought patterns, we will keep returning to this mental set point until we bring some awareness to the patterns we are trying to change.

The fire that drives you

Without action, there are no results, and without desire, there can be no action. Ambition is the fire that drives your desire for career success. Let's look at two different career path options – one is the path you are on, which will continue the way it is unless you do something about it. And I'll assume since you picked up this book, that you are interested in making your career more awesome than it is right now. The other path is your new career trajectory, which is more satisfying, meaningful and engaging. Be wary of linking ambition to greed, because you may end up sabotaging your success. Take a second to look around you: the seat you are sitting in, the buildings around you, the country you live in, are all the result of someone's ambition. As you will learn in Chapter 9, it pays to seek career challenges for your future self. And your future self will have more skills, confidence and connections than you do today, so bigger ambition will be within your grasp to accomplish. Never limit your ambition based on your current competency. A key component of ambition is contribution. What do you want to give to others or give back? Another component of ambition is connection with others. We will go deeper into relationship strategy in Chapter 8, but it all starts with your ambition to build amazing relationships and improve your existing relationships.

Many people are hungry at the beginning of their careers for some level of success, and then when they achieve that, they relax, they stop progressing, and they lose ambition. If you have ambition, you can find the solutions you need for your career – the right skills, strategy, support, etc. So how do you sustain hunger? How do you keep your ambition alive?

Sometimes it's a big birthday, a sign that you are aging, a medical crisis, or the birth of your first child that reignites your drive. This might sound morbid, but contemplate your own mortality. When you get to the end of your life, what will you ask yourself? Will you be satisfied that you have used your time on earth to your best ability? The good news is that humans are naturally ambitious, curious and driven beings, but we can get derailed with failure or people telling us we can't succeed. If you have lost your ambition, ask yourself how you lost it. If you have lost your ambition, you may not be connecting with something larger than yourself that pulls you, and being pulled towards something is so much easier than pushing yourself to have to do something. You can't be ambitious just because you feel like you should be.

Who you are

Our thoughts, actions, patterns, success, etc. come from who we are being. Think about that for a second. This means you don't have to change a million things to get to where you want to go in your career, you just have to change who you are being. If, going into a meeting, I can have a huge to-do list: smile, be friendly, be confident, talk smoothly, remember to compliment people, etc, and as soon as I place my focus on one, I forget to do another. This is the hard way (sometimes you have to change your behaviour the hard way to hardwire it). There is also an easy way. All those behaviours will flow naturally from you, if are showing up as a person who gives compliments and leads the room and is confident.

Ron Malhortra, business coach and founder of The Successful Male movement in Australia told me that the first thing we need to do to have a successful career is to find out who we are. And deep down, we all want to know who we are. We want to know if we have what it takes when faced with the biggest challenges and peak moments of our lives. As you know, I'm all about adventure, and I think it is the best tool to find out who you are. Adventure means placing yourself in all kinds of unfamiliar situations where you have to rely on yourself to make it through. Adventure is a grand self-experiment to see how you respond when the going gets tough.

What is the foundation for who you are? In our interview, coach and author Christine Hassler told me that the qualities that you embody doing the things that you love is who you truly are. For example, when I am exploring in the jungles of Bali, I am being passionate, excited, brave, resourceful, curious and present, to name a few. And we have different versions of ourselves that show up at different times. When you are hanging out with your best friends you are different than when you are meeting your partner's parents for the first time or when you are leading a board meeting.

We all have our blind spots as well – we can observe ourselves closely, but we can't see everything. The good news is that you are surrounded by friends, colleagues, family, bosses, etc who also notice things about you. Good feedback is important, so ask what they see in you. Who do you show up as according to them? What do they think are your best qualities and biggest weaknesses? Where do they see you playing small, and what potential do they see for you?

Energy foundations

Use your body

Your mind is your most powerful tool in your career, but don't forget it is part of your physical body. Getting into detail about your health is beyond the scope of this book, but you need to be doing everything you can to cultivate a strong physical foundation, in order for your mind to perform at its best. I like to think about energy as both physical and mental energy. Physical energy gives you the stamina to focus for long hours and mental energy keeps you hungry.

We will learn in Chapter 7 how the body and mind are connected. You can change how you feel simply by moving your body. Big postures that take up space (called power posing) can boost your testosterone and reduce cortisol. Animals physically shake to reduce stress. After a wolf has chased an antelope, the antelope will shake its body to reset its physical state. Humans have this same ability too!

Have you heard the Taylor Swift song, 'Shake It Off'? When we don't take advantage of it, the stress response internalizes and lives in our tissues – this is why your shoulders get tense during a hard day at work and why a massage makes you feel so relaxed.

Get stoked!

Each year, I conduct an annual review and give the upcoming year a theme. Brendan Leonard, the adventure writer, inspired me to make 2018, 'The year of being stoked.' Stoked is when you take enthusiasm, joy and excitement about what you are doing and you take it to the extreme. In our interview, we talked about how some adventure buddies make a trip so much better by how they show up. Leonard told me that 'You are way more likely to succeed in climbing a big wall rock climb and have more fun and energy doing it when your climbing partner brings the stoke'. You get to decide if you are going to be stoked or grumpy, so why not be stoked?

Like many people, when I first got to college, I decided to reinvent myself. For some reason I decided that I was going to be a pirate (I guess pirates were cool at the time, because the next year the film *Pirates of the Caribbean* came out). Anyway, I decided that I would be a swashbuckling character who didn't care about the rules and could do what I wanted. This made me feel confident and excited and independent. I tell you this to illustrate that I decided to feel a certain way and then I did it. We have all had situations where we want to be brave or joyful and we let ourselves embody those feelings. This means we have the ability to control how we feel.

How you feel controls your energy levels. If you feel joyful, your most difficult challenges will be welcome, but if you feel depressed, those challenges are insurmountable. If you feel irritable, collaborating with your team or strategic networking will be the last thing you will want to do.

What feelings give you the most energy? I was talking with a client recently who told me she wanted to feel wild and free again like when she was younger. She also wanted to leave behind some negative thought loops. We decided that whenever she felt unhappy or upset, she would revert back to being positive, wild and free.

EXERCISE – Determine how you want to feel

Everything we do, we do because we are chasing a certain feeling. Pick the top three ways you want to feel on a daily basis.

Environment

What surrounds you in your environment leads your thoughts. This includes people as well as your home, your possessions, what you read, conversation you have, and what part of the world you live in. This is your diet of thoughts and experiences. We want to carefully curate the world in which we place ourselves to optimize for the career and life we are trying to have.

Your physical environment is so important. Have you heard of Feng Shui before? Feng Shui is the Chinese thought that takes into account the flow of energy when designing buildings and rooms. Author Marie Kondo wrote *The Life Changing Magic of Tidying Up* – where she helps people manage their environments to help them be happier and more efficient (Kondo, 2014). Kondo says if you put your hand on an object and it sparks joy, you may keep it, otherwise thank it for its service and get rid of it. When you declutter your physical space, you also supposedly declutter your mind. For a nomadic entrepreneur like me, it's easy to keep your possessions to the most valuable few – you can only carry one or two bags on the airplane when you go to a new continent. I try to only buy things that I know I will love to use for more than 15 years, so I don't have to purge anything later. It will be an interesting challenge when I finally have a house big enough to display my collection of cultural artefacts from my travels. I will likely have to have a 'museum room' for the hundreds of art objects I have acquired from around the world.

In the book *Geography of Bliss*, Eric Weiner searches for the happiest places on earth. What he found is that people's surroundings profoundly influenced their happiness (Weiner, 2008). Moldova was one of the least happy countries in the world, largely because people felt they had no control over their destiny. Whereas people in Switzerland were surrounded by beautiful scenery, had enough money, had choices about their future, and their trains run on time. Weiner remarked 'Culture is the sea we swim in – so pervasive, so all-consuming, that we fail to notice its existence until we step out of it. It matters more than we think.'

I have lived in dozens of different countries around the world. I know that it is important for me to have close access to nature. Ideally I have hiking and biking trails right outside my front door, but in many cities this isn't possible, so I have to make sure I know how to get into nature quickly. I also know that I do not like to commute by car to work, so I have never taken a job that was more than 15 miles away from my house, so that I could commute by bicycle. Even in the below zero temperatures of St Paul Minnesota, I was able to operate without owning a car.

Later, in Chapter 8, we will look at optimizing the people we surround ourselves with. Jim Rohn famously said: 'You are the average of the five people you spend the most time with' (Groth, 2012). If you watch the news, the fear mongering and sensationalism will be your input to conversation. If you hang out with runners, like I did in college, your conversation will be heavily weighted to running. The inputs from the conversations you have and the information diet you are on will profoundly influence your thoughts.

Resilience

Our ability to be effective in our career is contingent on our ability to function. We lose productivity time to illness, which can't really be helped, but we can improve on how quickly we return from setbacks.

Disappointment often comes from having the outcome of events not match our expectations. This can mean that something didn't go according to plan, or it did go according to plan, but you don't feel like you thought you would, or life just throws you a complete curveball. When we have unmet expectations, we can be left with negative, lethargic feelings, or as Christine Hassler put it in our interview, an 'Expectation Hangover'. One way to remedy this is by creating agreements instead of expectations. So if you are managing an employee and you want a report back from them by noon on Friday, ask 'can we agree that you will get this to me by noon on Friday? Repeat that agreement back to me'. If you keep expecting something from someone (like encouragement from a parent) but they never give it to you, it might be time to go and seek that from another place. Christine Hassler put it this way, 'If you really want nachos, you aren't going to go to a Chinese restaurant'.

Thailand is one of the happiest countries in the world, but they do not pursue happiness directly, rather their happiness comes from a focus on living in the present moment. What does this mean for us to pursue our career ambitions? Hassler tells us that we must pursue our dreams with high intent, but low expectations. This means, throw your every effort behind your objective, but given the infinite number of possible outcomes, don't get caught up expecting one thing or another.

If you do get an expectation hangover, you may be filled with negative emotions. When you can observe these emotions without judgement, you have a much better chance of processing them without getting stuck on them. This means you have to be willing to feel the emotions that make you physically or intellectually uncomfortable. The important part when we deal with an expectation hangover is that most people want to get through the negative feelings quickly and don't take time to explore their response.

Our goal is to reduce the severity of the negative emotions and the frequency that you experience expectation hangovers.

EXERCISE – Understand your thoughts

Fast forward to the free-writing exercise in Chapter 3 for specifics on how this technique works. When you are experiencing thoughts and feelings you don't like, do a free-writing session – writing as fast as you can about those negative emotions. Then once you have got everything out and you feel a shift in your mood, feel free to burn the paper you wrote everything on. Then you will be in a freer and more open mood to write a second time and you can look clearly at your experience and what lessons are available to you. I learned from Life Athletics founder Nik Wood to always be asking, 'what am I supposed to learn from this?' about our challenging experiences.

Credibility foundations

Expert status

When I look at a job advertisement they often say something like 'bachelors degree and five years experience required'. Those requirements are not really accurate – they are simply a filter that is going to lead to candidates who are more likely to have the skills that enable them to do the job well. Employers don't hire you for your diploma, they hire you for the specific skills needed to do a job.

In a changing workforce, there are new careers being invented all the time that have no degree programme, and no way to earn relevant experience because they are brand new. So what you need to be able to do is build expert status for yourself, external to the previous system of university and organized credentials.

Expert status is the perception or reputation in your field that you are an expert at what you do. There are many indicators of being an expert: you have written a book in your field, been on TV, host a podcast, give talks, write a blog, participate in conferences, have customer testimonials, etc that all build the case for the observer that you are good at what you say you are good at.

Show your work

A career and body of work can only evolve by taking action. I love the book *Show Your Work* by Austin Kleon. He makes the case that we should be much more public with the things that we are creating (Kleon, 2014). If you are doing things that are good for the world, then you better not be hiding. The same goes if you are trying to make something big happen in the world – if no one can see you, you will not be influential enough to make big things happen.

Cultivate a bias towards finishing things. Author Scott Young told me that people were much more interested in his work once he had finished his first big challenge – completing the MIT computer science degree in just a single year instead of four (more on this in Chapter 5). Adventurers who I interview on the show have been able to become professional presenters and tell their story, only after they have achieved great feats of endurance, speed or exploration.

Your personal brand

During my bicycle racing days, I worked at a bike shop in my hometown of St Louis, called the Hub. This was a new bicycle store in a city with many bike shops already and facing competition from internet sales. But the cofounders succeeded in growing their revenue and customer base every year – why? Because they leveraged their established personal brands from working in other bike shops in the area. When they opened their store, loyal customers followed them over. New customers stay loyal because of the relationships that the owners build with each of them. These relationships are built around more than just bike knowledge – they are playful, full of random stories, wagers and shared beers.

Career and business strategist, Jenny Blake, put it to me this way: in the restaurant industry, cooks are almost a commodity and succumb to the whims of the market, but chefs who have built a reputation will always have opportunities available to them. So right now, whatever platform you choose, start sharing some strong opinions and talking about what you do. If your Facebook friends, or colleagues down the hall can't say exactly what you are good at, or know who to recommend you to for a job, then you haven't established your personal brand well enough. This is becoming the age of the personal brand. As I write this, the Facebook algorithm has been changed to favour personal content. That means if you want to drive income and interest through social media, you need to establish your unique brand. To understand your current brand, you may want to Google yourself. Buy YourName.com and start using Your Name@YourName.com for emailing. The most common error I see around personal branding is that people hide. They are not talking about what they do because it makes them uncomfortable, and they are uncomfortable because they are lacking conviction and sharing about themselves feels unfamiliar. We will work more on this in the storytelling chapter.

Foundational systems

If there is anything you are doing repeatedly in your career, you can free up time and cognitive power by investing in a system. People who get trapped doing the same things over and over and just trying to do it faster will ultimately limit themselves. If you can create a good system, you can ensure quality and creating more time. If you spend five hours teaching yourself all the keystroke shortcuts on your computer, and that saves you an hour a week, over the course of the year, you have a 1,000 per cent+ return on investment in time. If you teach your team how you want decisions made, they don't have to ask you each time, which saves time for everyone. In grad school I had a bioinformatics professor who was a real stickler about how we labelled our computer files. She wanted the same format for each project, because with 20 students, each submitting projects each week, she was dealing with a lot of files. This skill has saved me countless hours over the years because I can always find a document when I need it.

Your daily schedule is a system as well. You will learn about the costs of task switching in Chapter 4. We can save this mental cost by batching similar work. This means that instead of checking email throughout the day and responding as new emails arrive, you set aside a few (2–3) times per day to answer emails. John Lee Dumas releases one new episode of his podcast, Entrepreneur on Fire, every day, but he batches all the podcast interviews for the week on a single day. This means that the remaining days of his week are free to focus on other activities.

EXERCISE – Keep track of wins, and your success patterns

Create a notebook or document where you record every compliment on your work, testimonial, daily win and success story. Record what you did to achieve this success – the decisions you made, how you showed up. For long-term accomplishments, write through the experience step by step. Who were you serving? What was the impact of your accomplishment?

How did this success make you feel? When you look at all these wins, what common elements do they have? Which elements were crucial to your success? What patterns of success catch your attention? Are there any wins, big or small, that you did not record? Did you sell yourself short anywhere?

Conclusion

In this chapter we learned about the mental, energy and credibility foundations. When you combine these foundations with the skills in the remaining chapters of the book, you will find that they are easier to acquire and maintain. These foundations are the bare minimum that allow high performers to turn in excellent results year after year. The mental foundation is so important – setting you up to learn faster, be more creative, and manage your emotional state. Energy is what allows you to sustain a high-quality output over time. Establishing a credibility foundation allows you to leverage your past results for future opportunities.

Works cited

Bassham, L (1996) *With Winning in Mind: The mental management system – an Olympic champion's success system*, Bookpartners

Colvin, G (2015) *Humans Are Underrated: Proving your value in the age of brilliant technology*, Portfolio

Duhigg, C (2012) *The Power of Habit: Why we do what we do in life and business*, Random House

Goleman, D (1995) *Emotional Intelligence: Why it can matter more than IQ*, Bantam

Groth, A (2012, July 24) *You're the Average of the Five People You Spend the Most Time With*. Retrieved 25 February 2018, from Business Insider: www.businessinsider.com/jim-rohn-youre-the-average-of-the-five-people-you-spend-the-most-time-with-2012-7/?IR=T

Kleon, A (2014) *Show Your Work*, Workman Publishing Company

Kondo, M (2014) *The Life-Changing Magic of Tidying Up: The Japanese art of decluttering and organizing*, Ten Speed Press

Weiner, E (2008) *The Geography of Bliss: One grump's search for the happiest places in the world*, Black Swan

03
Optimizing your creativity

L ook around you: everything you see started as an idea. Someone designed the chair you are sitting in, made up the language you are reading this book in, and started the country you live in. Simply put, creativity is the way we come up with ideas. An Adobe Systems poll of 5,000 people across three continents reports that 80 per cent of people see unlocking creativity as key to economic growth. Yet only 25 per cent feel that they are living up to their creative potential (Adobe, 2012).

Creativity is a skill that enhances almost all other skills, and pairs really well with the other skills in this book. In this chapter, we are going to give you some practical tools and ways of thinking to immediately unlock your creativity, no matter what field you are in. We will also look at what holds people back from accessing their creativity – our pesky internal editor who makes us careful about how we share our creativity with the world. In our interview Mark Levy told me, 'I really find that one of the reasons why people don't come up with new ideas is they are scared of looking foolish. They also don't have tools with which to come up with new ideas.' On top of that, creativity can be hard work because you are thinking in ways that you don't normally think, which is why we need tools and frameworks for thinking creatively.

Once people are able to access their creativity, they enjoy it, but often their own view of their creative ability prevents them starting. Creativity is often relegated to the realm of artists, designers and writers. Meanwhile big important decisions are deemed to be decided in the boardroom. But companies such as Google and Facebook are changing the way we think about accessing each individual's creativity. Leaders in the tech and travel industries are, for example, building creative office cultures by introducing art into the workplace, encouraging employees to have a voice and suggesting new ideas for improving their company and getting their employees to improve their problem-solving skills by tackling novel projects (Lamb, 2015). Google engineers similarly get 20 per cent of their work time to spend on projects that interest them because it is believed that this will make them more productive at their main job (He, 2013).

There is a growing recognition in the business world that creativity leads to better results in the workplace. It is for instance reported that creativity improves productivity because it increases the motivation and passion of individuals and it encourages innovation and new approaches to problem solving (Jones, 2014). Even law firms are seeing the benefits of creativity to their bottom line. The skills of storytelling, empathy and vulnerability that underpin creativity help staff to better understand and communicate with clients (Himmelman, 2017).

Creativity is not just good for business; it is good for us. In fact, we are wired for creativity. Author of *Habits of a Happy Brain*, Loretta Breuning told me that creatively solving a problem triggers a release of dopamine in the brain – a neurochemical that gives us a feeling of happiness. This makes sense from an evolutionary perspective – our ancestors were rewarded for exploring new territory to find more food and expand their gene pool. In his book on *Flow and Creativity*, Mihaly Csikszentmihalyi reports that 'designing or discovering something new' is the feeling most often experienced during people's favourite activities, from rock climbing or playing chess (Csikszentmihalyi, 1996).

You might say 'Ideas alone don't make things happen,' and you would be correct. Execution is a subset of ideas. You can't make an idea happen without first having the idea. Here is an interesting way of framing it: American entrepreneur and author Derek Sivers says that ideas are just a multiplier of execution, and by themselves, ideas are worth nothing. For example, Sivers suggests that great execution is worth $1,000,000, and if you have a good idea you can multiply the value by 10. Creativity itself can only come through action, so you will need to set aside time to be creative and then use some of the ideas in this chapter (Sivers, 2005).

A creative adventure

Let's start with a story about how creativity brought together people of many different cultures.

I met Anne-Laure Carruth at the Travel Storytelling Festival and I was immediately intrigued by her story. Anne-Laure and her adventure buddy, Lucy Engleheart circumnavigated the Mediterranean by Land Rover, starting in England and driving through more than a dozen countries. Their mission was to collect stories of positivity and daily life along the way, especially from the Arab and North African countries, one of the fastest evolving cultural regions on earth.

Anne-Laure decided to do one drawing for every day of the trip. And because they were using a 1970 Land Rover that needed lots of maintenance, the team decided that the vehicle itself would become an art project. In each country, they partnered with local artists to 'pimp their ride'. Both Anne-Laure's drawings, the creation of an art vehicle 'Landy', and their interactions evolved along the way. Here are a few important creativity themes from their journey that we will discuss in more detail in this chapter:

- Creative constraints – they were defined by the form of the car.
- Creative consistency – it's easy to see the improvement in Anne-Laure's drawing throughout the journey as she showed up to create every day.
- Creative teamwork – without tapping into the local artists in each country, Landy would have never grown the personality it has today.

The beginners

In Chapter 2 we mentioned Carol Dweck's book *Mindset* as a mental foundation. How do fixed or growth mindset come into play with creativity? People with fixed mindsets believe their creative abilities are fixed and unchangeable, so there is no incentive to try new ways to be creative. With a growth mindset, you are free to try lots of things creatively – you are not bound by having to prove you are good at a certain style of creativity in order to use it (Dweck, 2006).

Every day with my son I am reminded of how children are willing to test and experiment multiple different ways of solving a problem. This is because they expect to be a beginner; they expect to not know how to do most things. If you have a healthy growth mindset, you may find yourself thinking like a beginner, even with familiar problems.

One of the fastest ways to drop yourself into a place of creativity is to move to a new country where the culture is totally different from your own. You are forced to drive on the other side of the road, speak a new language, try new foods, learn to bargain, etc. You are solving the problems of daily life all over again. If you can't go to a new country, go to hang out with a different group of people in your community, or take a class to learn a new skill and remind yourself what it is like to be a beginner. This is so great because it challenges your assumption that the way you have always done something is 'the right way'.

Be careful anytime you hear yourself say I'm right, or you are right. You can instead say – 'That is a better way of doing things', which leaves the possibility of still a better way that has yet to be discovered. I find that many solutions we see in the world are simply the first one that works and no one has bothered to improve them because they are 'good enough'. Whenever you find something that just isn't working smoothly – traffic flow, airport security, online banking – there is a ripe opportunity for innovation.

Separate the generation and evaluation of ideas

Three of the tools we will teach you in this chapter – brainstorming, mind mapping and freewriting – have one thing in common: no ideas are thrown out. We all have an internal editor that prevents us from saying something or writing something stupid. This is a useful mechanism for keeping us in good standing in our social group. What this cautious voice in our head is not good for is coming up with new and unique ideas. Luckily, with this awareness, we can avoid judging ideas while we are in the deep work of creating them. This can come from rules that are in place, or by working faster than the voice in our head can keep up.

Creative practice

It is often easier to come up with lots of ideas than one really good idea. In Claudia Azula Altucher's book, *Become an Idea Machine*, she talks specifically about the process of training your brain to generate lots of ideas and to use constraints to focus your idea generation (Altucher, 2015). Generating a multitude of ideas can build on each other and open up new patterns of thought. Altucher also talks about how ideas can lead to motivation. When you encounter lots and lots of ideas, the ones that really resonate with you and scream 'make me happen!' are your own million-dollar-ideas. Because execution is a multiplier of a good ideas, your own excitement around making something happen will greatly impact the eventual outcome.

> **EXERCISE – Be an idea generator**
>
> Each morning for one week, come up with 10+ ideas on a single theme. At the end of the week, you will have at least 70 ideas. Take a look and see what ideas might be applied from one realm to the next – explore the adjacent possible. What ideas can you give away that will help someone? Here are some prompts to get you started: 10 apps you could create, 10 people whose work you admire, 10 marketing ideas for your industry, 10 ways to save money in your business, 10 systems you could implement to save time… 10 your turn!

Creative confidence

In Chapter 8 we will learn all about charisma and confidence. In order to apply confidence to creative thinking, we need to develop our resilience around making mistakes, experiencing failure, and trying out bad ideas. On the Art of Adventure podcast that I produce and record, guests often talk about getting comfortable being uncomfortable or doing something every day that scares you. The Hungarian writer Gyorgy Korad said, 'Courage is only the accumulation of small steps' (Kelley, 2013). Stephen Pressfield talks often about 'the resistance' in his book *The War of Art*. The resistance is the feeling you get when you are dealing with an important idea that scares you a little bit (Pressfield, 2003). All this is to say that enhancing creativity is a daily practice that we can progressively master. Once you give yourself permission to be creative, then you become creative.

Your unique brand of creativity – multiple intelligences

The elementary school I attended based its curriculum on Harvard professor of education Howard Gardner's theory of Multiple Intelligences. The main intelligence types are (Gardner, 2000):

- musical-rhythmic and harmonic;
- visual-spatial;
- verbal-linguistic;
- logical-mathematical;
- bodily-kinaesthetic;
- interpersonal;
- intrapersonal;
- naturalistic;
- existential.

I won't get into the entire theory here, but the basics are that we all function with a combination of these intelligence types. For example, I was probably saved from ADD medication when my teacher realized that I was a kinaesthetic learner (I learn by moving), and she let me wander around the second-grade classroom, as long as I wasn't disrupting other kids. To this day, I continue to combine movement with learning. Some of my deepest philosophical discussions happen while cycling or running.

Gaining a good understanding of your predominant types of intelligence can help creating feel easier. For example, in recent years,

I have used a regular dance party to open up creativity prior to writing and speaking.

You can take free and quick self-assessments online to get a sense of what intelligences are more dominant for you. When you are choosing the direction you want to go for your career, it can be helpful to steer towards options that will allow you to use your primary intelligence regularly. If you are bodily-kinaesthetic like me, for example, you may feel more at home being a performer than a librarian. Linguistic intelligence might be great librarians, journalists or authors. Logical-mathematical people might consider finance, computer science or medicine.

If you are feeling frustrated in your career, consider adding elements that align with your predominant intelligences in your existing role. For example, if you are a manager and strong in naturalist intelligence, you may enjoy having team meetings while walking in a park. Remember that there is no one else in the world with your combination of intelligence style, skills and life experience. So you are a valuable addition to any creative endeavour.

Creative tool 1: how to brainstorm

Brainstorming is a valuable tool to generate great ideas and solutions to problems. I've been part of brainstorming sessions while developing new products at the 3M company and Napkin Labs, and nearly every day with my own business projects at the Art of Adventure. Brainstorming can be done on your own, but is best done with a diverse group.

Here are some guidelines for brainstorming that we will explore in detail:

- withhold any judgement of an idea;
- piggyback on others' ideas;
- keep coming up with ideas non-stop;
- stick to the topic at hand;
- go for wild and consider crazy ideas; and
- be visual if possible: draw or act out your idea.

Brainstorming has shaped the way I interact with people because of one of the principle tenets: don't throw out any idea. This means I will likely listen first and then be able to add to any conversation. Similarly, one of the key tenets of good improvisational comedy is the idea of 'Yes, and...', which we already know is a good practice for charismatic conversation. Withholding judgement of ideas begets more ideas than any other brainstorming rule.

Piggybacking on the other ideas is one of the greatest benefits of brainstorming sessions with a group. Good ideas naturally come from the little bits and pieces of ideas that are floating around. The easiest ideas are only a small step of understanding away from our current exposure. The more exposure to ideas, the more chances to make a leap or connection to create a new idea. This is why people who live in cities are 300 per cent more creative per capita than those that live in small towns – says Steven Johnson in his book *Where Good Ideas Come From*. With group brainstorming, tinkering with an idea, adding to it, and improving all in one session can save tons of time compared to a sole operator doing personal trial and error (Johnson, 2010).

If you keep coming up with ideas non-stop, you will eventually overcome the natural editor that each of us has waiting to nix saying something that is a little edgy or out of character. Rapid fire ideation also prevents you from thinking about what might not work. In fact, you should save the evaluation of the ideas for the post-brainstorming phase. Remember other people are counting on your volume of ideas in order to tweak their own and piggyback on.

Why encourage wild and crazy ideas when brainstorming? When people are asked to free associate, most fall under a normal bell curve of association. If you start with the colour blue the most common association is 'sky'. In a group where there were paid actors throwing out ridiculous and clearly false association, people's free association became more creative (Kelley, 2013). So in a brainstorming session, the wilder suggestions there are, the freer everyone's thinking becomes and a great many more creative ideas will result.

Finally, draw your ideas on the board. Circle parts of other ideas you like. Draw lines between ideas that you want to connect in a new thought. Use playdough to make a rough example of what you are trying to show. Get into character to better show a situation. Write in different colours. Use cartoons and weird symbols. Maybe I love brainstorming so much because the board ends up looking like a blend between the funny pages and a circus playbill.

EXERCISE – What would it be like if...

Here is a simple way to get your creative juices flowing before a brainstorming session. Come up with questions about an alternative reality, and let your imagine start to run wild. 'What would it be like if the world was like X...' If people could fly? If it rained money? If we all spoke the same language? If gravity switched halfway through each day?

Creative teams

One of my favourite companies in the world, IDEO is known for bringing together people with diverse backgrounds to form problem-solving teams. As with your personal network, your team should strive for age, cultural and career diversity. Each person brings different frameworks for thinking which can supplement each other's framework (Kelley, 2013). If you are a sole operator, get feedback: share your work and see what people react to. Often we can't predict what our best creative ideas will be until we see how they are received by others.

The rules of interaction for the team are as important as diversity. For example, I recently participated in an event called the 'House of Genius', where entrepreneurs can pitch their business idea, and get advice from a team of 'geniuses'. These geniuses are allowed to offer their advice for 60 seconds or less, and they are not allowed to share their last names or career experience until the end of the evening. Attendees can say +1 to agree with another idea and can piggyback quickly off ideas and topics. This framework means that everyone is focusing on the ideas and not status or how they will look to the others. In just half an hour, 20 experts who are focusing only on the problems of the entrepreneur in the hot seat can make substantial progress – I witnessed entire market pivots and re-working of app interfaces. Because you are not allowed to interrupt and the moderator keeps the pace moving fast, everyone must speak clearly and quickly. When you are running your own creative team sessions, consider having a leader or moderator and set up established rules.

Constrain your thinking

Narrowing your thinking can actually expand the potential ideas. Imagine a colouring book. You are limited by the lines on the page, but there are infinite ways to bring colour to the image. Author of *Accidental Genius* and consultant, Mark Levy, told me that instead of trying to come up with all possible ideas, use a narrow window of the type of idea you are going for. Start with the most outlandish possible limitations to force yourself to think differently.

Levy gave the example to try to come up with the worst idea possible. But within that, you can narrow your focus even more. Mark says: 'Let's look at different kinds of worst ideas. First, let's come up with all the really boring ideas that we possibly can. Just ideas that are screamingly boring. Then, how about a really dangerous idea? How about litigious ideas or how about ideas that are insanely expensive? What are ideas that would alienate women and what are ideas that would alienate men? What are ideas that would alienate children? All these would be separate buckets of ideas.'

He then goes on, 'Say you want to make a million dollars, okay. How would you make a million dollars in an hour? Let's say that you need to make a million dollars in an hour. Who is that going to be for? What is it that you could sell them, or make for them? You know, what are – and then okay if you can't do a million dollars in an hour how about a million dollars in a day? What would your million-dollar day look like, or your million-dollar week, or your million-dollar month. You know what I mean, and then we'd start playing in other directions too but I always try to get as concrete, and small, and literal as possible.'

Creative tool 2: mind mapping

Mind mapping is a tool used for visualizing a set of ideas. Instead of writing ideas in a list, ideas are spread across your page and can be given equal weight (again, helping separate the generation of ideas with the assessment of ideas).

My friend Caroline Weiler is the founder of Visual Story Mapping. When she was developing the concept, she sat down with me for a couple of hours and interviewed me about my life. The whole time she was mapping down important concepts and themes on the paper. We were able to start to see themes and patterns emerge in the major decisions I was making in life. One of our great abilities as humans is pattern recognition (how we started to see constellations in the stars many centuries ago).

Now, every time I begin a new project or business venture, I start off with a mind map. I look at all the different aspects – the business model, the niche, the clients, the market, the team, the execution strategy, etc. We get it all down on paper and we can truly understand the big picture. It helps us get clear on what points will be important – where is the leverage going to be? What is really valuable and where might we get tripped up?

Creative tool 3: free writing

I discovered free writing while I was in graduate school for microbiology as a way to understand my thoughts about my research. Mark Levy explains the name: 'It is called free writing as in free from the normal rules of writing. The normal rules of writing say that your writing is to communicate to other people. In free writing, it's to watch yourself think. It has nothing to do with other people.'

'I have to start reaching. I have to start putting together ideas that don't normally go together. I have to start thinking up stuff that I don't normally think about, and access different parts of my mind.'

EXERCISE – Your first free write

Sit down and set a timer for 10 minutes. Pick a topic you want to focus on. Write as fast as you can without stopping.

> ### EXERCISE – Blurt it out
>
> This is a two-person exercise that Mark Levy writes about in *Accidental Genius* in a chapter called, 'Help others do their best thinking' (Levy, 2010). Levy says he learned the exercise from a book called *How to Have Kick-Ass Ideas* By Chris Barez-Brown (Barez-Brown, 2008). This problem-solving activity allows you to go through a problem-solving cycle in 15 minutes and bypass your internal editors.
>
> Person A speaks as fast as they can about a current problem they are working on.
>
> Person B then has five minutes to respond with what they heard person A say and their suggested solutions.
>
> Finally, Person A has two minutes to respond to how their thinking has changed and what they might try to solve the problem.

Movement and creativity

Jono Lineen walked 5,000 miles across the Himalayas and wrote a book about his experience. But it took him 12 years and many revisions of the book to fully understand the purpose of his journey. Originally he thought it was to understand the culture, geography and spiritual traditions of the area. Eventually he realized the walk was a way for him to process the untimely death of his younger brother.

Lineen realized that the act of walking was a meditative experience that helped him deal with the deeper emotional issues that were affecting him. Walking allows us to access deeper ideas and truths that we can't normally access. Some of my most important life decisions have happened while hiking. This happens because the relaxing environment allows your daydreams and inner dialogue to wander more freely. Exercise can also release the flow of dopamine, which is a key ingredient for creativity. Movement may also distract people from focus on ineffective solutions (Widrich, 2013; Smith, 2016). The same thing happens when you're riding a bicycle, or doing other movement activities that don't take active concentration. You're also experiencing this when you're being struck by a great idea while in the shower. You can deliberately use walking or another type of movement when you're feeling stuck to boost your creativity.

Relaxed attention

Another benefit to walking is that it allows you to have relaxed attention on a problem. The book *Daily Rituals* examines the routines of creative individuals throughout history from scientists and painters, to philosophers and writers. Many of these great thinkers would work hard at their creative pursuit in the morning and take long walks after lunch or multiple times throughout the day. By leaving a problem, you create emotional distance between yourself and the problem that has been occupying your thoughts. The afternoon catnap or morning wake-up period can also provide this type of mental space (Currey, 2013).

EXERCISE – Creative mindfulness

In our interview, Jono Lineen proposed a form of walking mindfulness practice: think of a problem you are attempting to solve. Hold it in your mind while you walk. As soon as you notice your attention has drifted away, simply bring it back again to focus on the challenge, the same way you might return to a focus on your breath during mindfulness meditation (Lineen, 2015).

Follow your curiosity

I've grown my business on the back of asking questions. Before I was a podcaster, I was a scientist, where I asked different types of questions. In the book *Curious Mind*, film producer Brian Grazer talks about how asking questions of interesting people led to some of his best films, including *Apollo 13*, *A Beautiful Mind* and *8 Mile* (Grazer, 2015). In your career, you can get curious about your colleagues, employees and managers. Getting people to reflect on their work can give you insight into better ways you can collaborate with and help them. You can also build connection with people in your company by showing interest in their lives.

In business, it is so important to understand your client, or the end user of your product. One of the first things I often have clients do is market-research interviews – conversations with real people to understand exactly what they struggle with in specific areas. Once you hear what language people are using, and what problems come up over and over, people are often excited to find an a-ha moment pops into their mind. Doing these interviews can help you get out of your own thought patterns and see what other people are thinking.

Creative environments

Another important consideration in creative output is where you choose to practise creativity. People are more creative the larger the space they are working in, because their mental space is correlated to the mental expansiveness they feel (Rattner, 2017). Workers experience less stress and mental fatigue when nature is present (Groves, 2013). The halls of most elementary schools are covered in art, murals, sculptures, quotes, and interesting things of all kinds. This gives kids a constant exposure to new ideas and frameworks of thinking. When writing this book, I would often visit ancient libraries in European cities and let the centuries of learning inspire me.

I interviewed Travis Sheridan, the global director of development of Venture café, about how he creates conditions to 'connect innovators to make big things happen'. His goal with the weekly networking event is to use an open space, beer, workshops and proximity to start-up offices to attract a diverse crowd and increase the potential of cross-discipline chance encounters.

When you are thinking about running an event, think about the value that will attract your attendees, and make it as easy as possible for them to participate. Venture café has a built-in value because there are people there with opportunities and ideas for you. The free workshops are an ethical bribe to entice people. The free beer and mentorship from experienced volunteers make it less scary to attend. Everyone knows what to expect because the event runs at the same time and place every week.

Steal like an artist

In one of my favourite books, *Steal Like an Artist,* the author Austin Kleon discusses how artists find inspiration. I loved the story of how *Tonight* Show Host David Letterman set out to imitate Johnny Carson, and wound up as David Letterman (Kleon, 2012).

Have you ever heard a song and thought 'I don't like this as much as the version I know', only to find that you had been listening to a cover and assumed it was the original?

In business, some of our favourite products are 'stolen ideas' or new versions of something already on the market. The iPod, for example, was not the first MP3 player on the market, but it was the first one made by Apple.

In my daily routine, I often start my morning with 30 minutes of reading non-fiction in an area I'm excited to explore. This provides me with exciting new ideas that I can explore when I create podcasts, videos, coaching curriculum and book chapters.

As we'll see in Chapter 4, passion develops over time by increasing expertise. When it comes to creativity, we grow into the artist or creative version of ourselves only through testing things out.

Solve your own problems

When I started the Art of Adventure podcast, I knew that I wanted to meet and learn from explorers, adventurers, entrepreneurs and interesting people all over the world, so I simply created the podcast that I wanted to listen to. Luckily I am not so unique, and other people are also interested in business, travel and adventure.

When I thought about what type of trip I would pay to go on, I realized I wanted to combine physical adventures with growing my business, so I created AdventureQuest Travel. When you have intimate familiarity with a certain set of problems, it is much easier for you to come up with creative solutions around those problems.

The adjacent possible and the power of polymaths

Polymaths, otherwise known as generalists, can often feel frustrated by modern society's tendency to pigeonhole people into 'types' or specializations. I interviewed Patricia Parkinson on why having a diverse range of interests led to enhanced creativity. She told me that polymaths have access to ideas at the intersection of their interests, which specialists would never experience. Stephen Johnson calls this accessing the adjacent possible – by taking knowledge from one field and applying another way of thinking, we can generate entirely new types of ideas. As we saw in Chapter 5, having multiple frameworks of thinking helps you link new ideas more quickly. It also helps you translate ideas from one discipline to the next.

It can be helpful to bring on advisors with different ways of thinking. In *Smartcuts,* Shane Snow tells the story of a hospital that brought in a Formula One car racing pit crew to help figure out how it could have faster turnaround times in its emergency surgery section. The Formula One team is used to thinking about changing tyres and refuelling in a matter of seconds, and they will be aware of the physics and special requirements for efficient movements (Snow, 2014). If you want to bring in different experts for your own project, consider people that have experience with processes or technology tangentially related to your objectives. In the search for a lost city in Honduras, archaeologists wanted to survey large tracts of dense jungle and asked military surveillance for their expertise in Lidar LASER surveying (Preston, 2017).

Setting aside time in your schedule for hobbies, side projects and exploring new fields is important. This gives you the fuel for combinatory creativity.

Showing up

You may have heard that many authors experience something called writer's block. This is a symptom of a combination of a lack of motivation to do your work, because it does not interest you enough, and the gap between where your skills are and where you know they could be. Some people might claim to be perfectionists and wait and wait to produce their work. But a true perfectionist knows that perfection comes from the feedback and response you get from releasing your work.

Many of the best authors (Stephen King – 54 novels and 200+ short stories), musicians (The Beatles – wrote nearly 200 songs between 1962 and 1970), architects (Frank Lloyd Wright – designed more than 1,000 structures), and artists (Picasso – more than 50,000 works of art in his lifetime) are prolific creators. Simply by the law of probability, you will create more masterworks if you create more works overall. Combine prolific creation with feedback that leads to accelerated improvement (deliberate practice), and you increase your odds again of creating excellent creative output. Since our goal is also quality output you want to determine what output is most celebrated and advantageous in your field – how will your success be measured by your chosen field?

Imagine you are in the Matrix

I see over and over again in my clients and other entrepreneurs – they have an idea and for some reason they think, 'I'm not allowed to do that'. They have some made-up rules in their head about what is allowed. Jason Zook, creator of Iwearyourshirt.com made over $1 million wearing t-shirts with brand logos on them. He told me that his creative thinking was opened up by asking 'What if I was in the Matrix?' In the Matrix, essentially anything is possible, so you are allowed to try anything. So just because wearing branded t-shirts for money had never been tried in this way, Zook continued the process by planning how to make it work, rather than dismissing the idea. In another outside-the-box idea, Jason sold his last name for a year to the highest bidder. He has been known previously as Jason Surfrapp, and Jason Headsets.com. Finally, Zook was able to sell sponsorships that would be displayed within the pages of his book *Creativity for Sale*. These ideas represent business opportunities that would not be possible with conventional thinking, or by paying attention to your internal editor.

> **EXERCISE – What would it be like if...**
>
> Here is a simple way to get your creative juices flowing before a brainstorming session. Come up with questions about an alternative reality, and let your imagination start to run wild. 'What would it be like if the world was like X...' If people could fly? If it rained money? If we all spoke the same language? If gravity switched halfway through each day?

Creativity is powerful

In many religious traditions, God is seen as the 'creator of all things'. If that is the case, then using our own creativity is a small reflection of the divine. It's a lot of responsibility and it's a lot of power. If your creativity does not have a productive outlet, it will find an outlet nonetheless. This is where criminal masterminds come from. Share your creativity! If you are not fulfilling your creative potential, you are robbing the world of your best work.

Works cited

Adobe (2012) *Global benchmark study on attitudes and beliefs about creativity at work, school, and home*, Adobe Systems

Altucher, C A (2015) *Become An Idea Machine: Because ideas are the currency of the 21st century*, Choose Yourself Media

Barez-Brown, C (2008) *How to Have Kick-Ass Ideas: Get curious, get adventurous, get creative*, Skyhorse Publishing

Csikszentmihalyi, M (1996) *Creativity: Flow and the psychology of discovery and invention*, Harper Perennial

Currey, M (2013) *Daily Rituals: How artists work*, Knopf

Dweck, C S (2006) *Mindset: The new psychology of success*, Random House

Gardner, H (2000) *Intelligence Reframed: Multiple intelligences for the 21st century*, Basic Books

Grazer, B (2015) *A Curious Mind: The secret to a bigger life*, Simon & Schuster

Groves, K (2013, 28 February) *Four types of space that support creativity & innovation in business*. Retrieved 26 February 2018, from Enviable Workplace: http://enviableworkplace.com/four-types-of-space-that-support-creativity-innovation-in-business/

He, L (2013) Google's Secrets of Innovation: Empowering its employees, *Forbes*

Himmelman, P (2017) Creativity: The strategic necessity you may not have thought of, *Forbes*

Johnson, S (2010) *Where Good Ideas Come From: The natural history of innovation*, Riverhead Books

Jones, B (2014) 5 Ways Creativity Leads to Productivity, *Entrepreneur*

Kelley, T K (2013) *Creative Confidence: Unleashing the creative potential within us all*, Crown Business

Kleon, A (2012) *Steal Like an Artist: 10 things nobody told you about being creative*, Workman Publishing Company

Lamb, L (2015) Inside the Creative Office Cultures At Facebook, IDEO, and VirginAmerica, *Fast Company*

Levy, M (2010) *Accidental Genius: Using writing to generate your best ideas, insight, and content*, Berrett-Koehler Publishers

Lineen, J (2015) Walking the heart of the Himalayas (D Loudermilk, Interviewer)

Pressfield, S (2003) *The War of Art: Break through the blocks & win your inner creative battles*, Warner Books

Preston, D (2017) *The Lost City of the Monkey God: A true story*, Grand Central Publishing

Rattner, D M (2017, 3 June) *How to Use the Psychology of Space to Boost Your Creativity*. Retrieved 26 February 2018, from How to Design Creative Workspaces According to Research: https://medium.com/s/how-to-design-creative-workspaces/how-to-use-the-psychology-of-space-to-boost-your-creativity-4fe6482ef687

Sivers, D (2005, 16 August) *Ideas Are Just a Multiplier of Execution*. Retrieved 26 February 2018, from Derek Sivers: https://sivers.org/multiply

Smith, J (2016, 14 January) 72% of people get their best
    ideas in the shower – here's why. Retrieved 26 February
    2018, from *Business Insider*: www.businessinsider.com/
    why-people-get-their-best-ideas-in-the-shower-2016-1/?IR=T

Snow, S (2014) *Smartcuts: How hackers, innovators, and icons accelerate
    success*, HarperBusiness

Widrich, L (2013, 28 February) *Why We Have Our Best
    Ideas in the Shower: The science of creativity*. Retrieved 26
    February 2018, from Buffer: https://blog.bufferapp.com/
    why-we-have-our-best-idcas-in-the-shower-the-science-of-creativity

04
Do your best work

If you want to be valuable in any career, you want to do your best work. The hard part is figuring out which work to do, and then maximizing your ability to do more high-quality work.

What makes an incredible career in your field? Are you spending time doing work that seems urgent but really isn't important? Do you feel like you can never catch up with your endless to-do list?

If your current career does not often require you to do your best work, then you are likely in a career that is not valuable in the economy of the future. If you're not doing your best work then it's a sign that your job could be done by someone else or not even needed in the future.

When I was working as a food safety microbiologist doing repetitive experiments, I realized that it would only take a few days to train a recent college graduate to do the same work. My only competitive advantage was that I could do these tasks slightly faster. This was a dangerous place to be, and when the economy collapsed in 2008, I was one of the first people let go.

What this chapter is about

You need to be able to produce high-quality work in high quantity. So how do we swing for the fences, make the best possible work, and create consistently? In this chapter we will think about the small number of things that make the biggest difference in your career, the power of doing work that brings you satisfaction and meaning. We will teach you to think about your work like a fine craftsman, which is much harder to automate.

One of the most important things to figure out in any career is which work has the most impact on your overall success. If you are going to be an author, it's writing books. It's not mastering Instagram or tweaking your website even though these things might be important to building your profile as an author. Focusing your time on what's going to create success is key and we will help you determine what are the most important outcomes from your work that you should be prioritizing each day.

We will talk about energy. It is your brain that is producing great value. Investing in the environment and your physical body that allows your brain to run at its maximum capacity is key. We will talk about willpower and daily routines that set us up for success in producing high-quality work.

Cal Newport calls the ability to focus without distraction on cognitively demanding tasks 'deep work'. This means doing what you are most valuable doing, creating something new for the world, problem solving and maximizing the output of your efforts and time.

Our workplaces often feature open office floor plans, regular meetings and constant electronic connectivity, all of which detract from our ability to do our best work. We live in a distracted world and one where there are constant bombardments to our attention. Attempts to multitask, or frequently switch tasks, can lead to a loss of productivity by up to 40 per cent and an increase in errors (Weinschenk, 2012). Because this level of distraction affects everyone, those who can rise above the noise to carve out time and to do their best work will have a competitive advantage over others in any career path and employment market.

Again, one of the main themes of this book is that we want to target doing something that is uniquely human, using your brain to the best of its ability, rather than doing something like answering emails, which could be automated by the right artificial intelligence. Beware the trap of busy-ness.

We will also talk about focus. Being able to concentrate intensely is a skill that requires practice. It can be frustrating when you are 'out of shape'. But if you actually do the work and train your ability to concentrate, then you will have a huge advantage over people that do not do this – it becomes like a superpower.

Finally, we will help you get more time by investing in systems and practices that can free up your valuable time.

First, let's start with a story of what doing your best work might look like.

What my best work looked like five years ago

When I was in grad school for Microbiology I needed to present my master's thesis (give a scientific lecture) and then defend the thesis in private in front of my committee. The thesis itself was 75 pages and had taken me six months to write. I practised the talk about 20 times in the few months leading up to the final defence.

To prepare for the talk, I practised in front of my advisor, my colleagues, by myself in the mirror and with a video camera. I learned the gaps in my presentation so I had to go back to the laboratory and do brand new experiments for weeks. I let other PhD students grill me on ideas and I reviewed all the exams from my course work. I listened to podcasts about how to deliver a speech and I studied videos about body language and charisma.

Before the talk I spent hours preparing my mindset by doing exercises to boost my confidence, because I knew I would need to be at the top of my mental game for at least four hours. During the talk I slowed down, made eye contact, moved about the room and engaged with the audience. After the public presentation, we moved to a closed-door session with just me and three of the top scientists in my field. Over several hours, my committee grilled me, asking me harder and harder questions. It is well known that the committee will try to make you lose composure. But luckily, I had prepared for this by asking people who had successfully passed their defence about how to respond. For things that I didn't know, I told them how I would find out and what I thought would need to be done next.

At the end of this process, I was utterly worn out and could hardly think straight. Even though I had come well prepared, I stumbled frequently while answering hard questions and thought that it was possible I would not pass. Later, when the committee told me I had successfully defended, they said it was one of the best presentations and defence they had ever participated in (sounding surprised).

I tell you this story to illustrate how a single successful result came from years of research, careful preparation, concentration, quality feedback, focus, purpose and planning – many of the concepts that we will dive into in this chapter.

What is the most important work?

Deciding what to do each day is important. We all have the same amount of time, yet some people achieve phenomenal results. What are they doing differently than the average person? Highly productive people are often prolific creators and they are also producing quality output. There are a few key ideas in this section – the 'Lead Domino' and the 80/20 rule.

Using the 80/20 rule or Pareto's principle – what 20 per cent of activities will lead to 80 per cent of the results for a successful career in your field? In other words, what will make you a star in your field?

The first time I made $50,000 in a week, I slowed down and only did a couple things each day. I focused on the only thing that I needed to do to make money – have conversations with potential clients.

The idea of the 'lead domino' is the one thing that by doing it makes all other things easier. In many areas, this can be making sales. Then you are generating more income and getting more customer interaction that inform the future direction of your business. Sometimes the lead domino can be key partnerships or marketing efforts that open the right door for you. Sometimes the lead domino can be addressing your own energy and motivation, to allow you to work consistently.

Often, we can recognize the lead domino because it is a challenging task that gets put off and moved over from yesterday's to-do list. Resistance comes from things that are going to challenge us, that generate discomfort and fear. The first place to look for your lead domino is what you have been putting off.

After completing your successful morning routine, I suggest that you schedule your lead domino activity first thing. This way, if you need to respond to things that come up throughout the day, or lose energy, or overestimate your time commitments, then at least you will finish the day satisfied with completing your most important activity.

Determining prolific quality output

In his book *High Performance Habits*, Brendon Burchard introduces the idea of Prolific Quality Output (PQO) (Burchard, 2017). Academic and author of numerous self-improvement books, Cal Newport, told me that the key metric of quality output in his field of science was publishing papers in well known scientific journals. So, even though he does other things like writing self-help books, he needs to make getting papers published in scientific journals a priority.

You need to determine the PQO for your own career – what outputs will make you more effective, better known, and better remembered? It may be helpful to model the careers of people at the elite level in your field to work out what your PQO is. Do some research to find out what they did to get where they are now and then follow their lead.

Once you know your PQO, those activities often become your lead domino and can be scheduled into the beginning of your day. But sometimes it is not clear what it will take to accomplish a large project. So it is helpful to break down a little further and ask what are the major waypoints to creating this particular PQO. In the case of writing this book, finishing the book would be the first waypoint. Promoting the book is another important waypoint.

Meaning and motivation

Daniel Goleman tells us in his book *Focus* that it takes less willpower for us to do work that we love (Goleman, 2013). If your work reflects your passions and purpose, it becomes effortless. If you spend your time doing meaningful activities at work and outside of work, you end the day feeling fulfilled and begin the next with more excitement. Regularly checking in with what brings you meaning and what things you are looking forward to can cue you towards more valuable activities and away from meaningless distraction such as channel or web surfing.

Simon Sinek has a famous TED talk and book about starting with 'Why'. Why are you bothering to do the hard work you are doing? What are your goals in life? How do you want to feel, what do you want to create, and how does an effort to do your best work align with those values? Often, when my clients are struggling with motivation or feel overwhelmed – they get lost in the day-to-day operations of running their business – I have them come back to their vision for why they started the business in the first place. It can be helpful to clearly articulate your goals with some sort of map, vision board, or manifesto that you can physically display on the wall of your work space.

Deep work

I interviewed Cal Newport about his book *Deep Work*. He told me that some of the rarest and most valuable work that happens in the world today is performed in distraction-free concentration, where we are pushing our cognitive ability to its limit. This is another activity that cannot be replaced by robots or AI. By contrast, shallow work can be repetitive, done in a distracting environment, does not create new knowledge in the world, and is easy to outsource or replicate.

There are two parts to optimizing deep work: understanding what the most important work you should be doing is, and setting up your daily schedule to maximize your ability to do those challenging tasks in a focused way. Part of deep work is the ability to learn hard things quickly (see Chapter 5 on accelerating how you learn).

If you are attempting to think about a complex problem, or trying to learn a challenging new skill, you are using too many different brain circuits in the brain to fully allow the circuits you wish to strengthen.

Grit

Education theorist Tom Hoerr told me that one of the most important traits we can foster is grit – the ability to persevere when we are challenged. Researcher Angela Duckworth defines grit as, 'working strenuously toward challenges, maintaining effort and interest over years despite failure, adversity, and plateaus in progress' (Duckworth, 2016). In a group of equally talented individuals, level of grit may be the greatest predictor of success. If we are working to improve and become more valuable in the marketplace, it is inevitable that we will run into walls and hit failure points. And when we do, we need to be able to move past that without getting stuck. You can develop your own grit by choosing to persevere when things get tough and by having a coach or a peer that keeps you accountable to your goals. A successful leader will surround themselves with the right people that can help them push through obstacles when they come up.

Morning routine

We know that humans are cognitive misers – we can only make a certain number of hard decisions before we need to rest and recharge. Setting up a daily routine can help you arrive at your important tasks with maximum willpower and concentration. Having a morning routine that you go through every work day can automate this process. Additionally, many people check their email or social media upon waking. This can put us in a responsive state, where we feel we are not in control of our day.

In the book *The Miracle Morning*, Hal Elrod proposes a morning routine that brings you to the start of your workday with the right mindset to tackle objectives (Elrod, 2012). I've taken that framework and expanded it through careful experimenting. Here are the main elements that I help my clients include in their morning ritual. Each of these can be done for 5–30 minutes, depending on how much time you have to invest in the morning:

- *Meditation or silence.* A simple body scan meditation such as Kelee meditation is often effective. This segment of the routine often includes breathing exercises that change the body's pH levels. (I recommend the Wim Hof method or breath work for those who want to go deeper.)

- *Journaling*. This is where you plan your day and reflect on the previous day's effort. Questions to journal about: What are three things I am grateful for? What would make today great? How do I want to feel today? What were three great things from yesterday?

- *Movement or exercise*. I recommend doing this first, along with drinking two glasses of water. Movement is better than coffee for waking up your body. Movements that stretch major muscle groups and bouncing exercises are the most effective. You can do a four-minute Tabata protocol with eight movements (20 seconds of intense movement, 10 seconds rest).

- *Read* relevant or inspirational non-fiction (I suggest *Superconductors*!). From the chapters on creativity and learning, you know that our ability to link ideas and move into the adjacent possible is important, so start your day with new knowledge input.

- *Affirmations*. These are simple statements that cue you in to how you want to show up that day or depicts the version of your best self that you want to be. This can include how you relate to others, how you live from your values, or traits about yourself that you want to highlight. You can also use or read aloud from an inspiring speech or written passage – something that brings you to speak passionately out loud.

- *Visualize*. We know from mental performance training and Olympic athletes that visualizing is one of the best ways of improving our skill at any activity. This can be in the form of rehearsing a physical skill, or understanding what your day's meetings and tasks will look like. As you visualize, see yourself completing the activity in the way that you want to complete it. Also visualize the order of activities throughout the day. You can be on the lookout for potential pitfalls by asking yourself – where might I get stuck today?

Daily schedule

High-quality work is a matter of both focus and time spent, so it is important for us to look carefully at how we spend our time each day. There are a few different types of scheduling strategies that will enable you to set aside distraction-free work time. One option is to set aside a block of time each day and always show up and do your focused work at the same time – for example, immediately after your morning routine. Another option is to leave your normal schedule for days or weeks at a time to crank out focused work. You may decide you need to drop everything and spend a year living as a hermit in the woods. Or if you have a kid like me, you may sometimes need to be flexible and drop into your concentrated work as the time arises in your schedule.

In the book *Daily Rituals* (Currey, 2013), about history's greatest creators and geniuses, there were two main trends that I observed for how creatives structure their day to create their best work. It appears that many successful people have a chunk of time, usually in the morning, where they will bust out three or four hours of high-quality work. People like Einstein and Mark Twain used this method. If you follow this approach you choose the best time of day to focus on your most creative work and then spend the rest of your day doing tasks that don't need as much concentration such as responding to emails, networking and posting on social media.

The other style of creativity, on the other hand, is linked to a more ad hoc schedule of sleeping in late, working late into the night, sometimes for 12 hours at a stretch, and working yourself into a state of fervour just to crank out the work. If you use this approach then you need to have the flexibility in your schedule to drop everything to complete a task.

As an example, some people can't fit concentrated work into their normal week and need to leave their daily lives for a moment and go to the country for a week and immerse themselves in deep for no distractions. I had many friends in Bali who would have to leave our town to get away from the constant onslaught of opportunities and go to quiet beach-side towns in the middle of nowhere to write.

Finding the right schedule that suits your creative style and your practical constraints will help you fit concentrated work time into your life.

Example: how I approach my workday while travelling

There are lots of important things that I am committed to doing each day: spending time with my son Axel, working on my business, spending time with my partner Heidi, supporting the needs of our house (chores), moving my body and staying healthy, connecting with the community in each new country we move to, and learning something new.

When you work from home it's really important to make sure you get focused work time. If I am creating new content three hours a day, that is a win for me. I can work the rest of the day on marketing, coaching, answering emails, networking, you name it. Cal Newport says one of the rarest and most valuable skills is the ability to focus deeply on creating something meaningful.

I make sure I set clear boundaries for what times are focus times to not be interrupted. This is especially important when I am doing coaching or recording podcasts. Sometimes I leave the house and work from a co-working space for a change of scenery. When you work from home, your home environment has to facilitate productivity.

I'm starting to realize why families love to move to the suburbs so that they can have lots of space – because they just want a little bit of quiet and the bigger the house you have, the more space you have to get away from noisy kids!

One advantage of working at home is that you can have your business pay for the part of your home you use as an office. You can also have the business pay for part of your internet and phone and meals and more, as long as these are in service of growing your business. Another big advantage is you can start work when you want. I haven't regularly woken up to an alarm in years.

For my work schedule, each morning when I do my morning journaling, I start with a basic to-do list. I look at what has been moved on from the day before, probably something that I have been avoiding because I have some kind of resistance to it. That's usually a good sign that it is important. I also look at what would most directly lead to income, since money is a lever that can be used to make all kinds of other things easier. You can buy time with money (an assistant, better equipment, a housekeeper, a nanny, etc).

If you are in an office, get out of your chair for a few minutes every hour to move around. If you are going from meeting to meeting, and checking things off your to-do list, you can close your eyes and take a deep breath – are you holding any tension anywhere in your body (for me it's the shoulders and jaw). Tell those muscles to relax and at the same time put the responsibility from the previous task on the shelf, so you can begin your next task with a clean slate.

Biological cycles and recovery

CEOs might as well be spending as much mental energy as Olympic athletes spend physical energy. They are making hard decisions and focusing all day long, and that takes lots of mental energy. We have already covered the foundation of energy, health and movement, so let's take a look at the importance of our natural biological rhythms and recovery process.

You might have heard of circadian rhythms – the biological system that controls your daily sleep/wake cycle. We also have shorter, roughly 90-minute cycles called ultradian rhythms that were first identified in sleep. These cycles continue through our whole day, not just while sleeping. Our brainwave frequency, energy levels and even body temperature ramp up and down throughout the day. How can we take advantage of these natural rhythms while we are working? By using a schedule that allows *alternating periods* of high-frequency brain activity (about 90 minutes) followed by lower-frequency brain activity (about 20 minutes) (Thibodeaux, 2017). When you feel sluggish or unmotivated, it might be time for a break. The theory is that your brain needs time to re-establish proper sodium/potassium ratios in your cells. You can also track which times of day you are most productive and engaged. You can plan to do your most important work during those times (Fallon, 2017).

Take your down time seriously. We all have the tendency to try to cram in a little more work or learning, even after we have just put in a lot of effort focusing for hours. But powering down the brain between challenges can help you bring your best effort during those challenges. I often force myself to take naps or go for runs where I don't listen to any music or podcasts. In *Deep Work*, Cal Newport suggests that we actively try to be bored sometimes (Newport, 2016) so that we are not training our brain to need constant distraction.

When I worked as a cycling coach, the number one thing I had to teach young athletes was how to rest and recover. If these athletes showed up too tired to do their most intense workouts effectively, they would not progress as fast as their peers who showed up fresh. Our body compensates and adapts to the training stress only when we allow it to fully recover between efforts. The same can hold true for your brain. If you push past the point of useful concentrated focus, your work may suffer the next day. I force myself to end my work day at least an hour before I plan to fall asleep. I spend time with my partner relaxing and chatting, often in the dark. I make sure I minimize screen time after sunset, because the blue light stimulates our brains, keeping us awake.

Eliminate distractions

The cost of shifting tasks is higher than you might think. According to Fast Company, if you interrupt your work, it takes an average of 23 minutes and 15 seconds to get back to the task (Pattison, 2008). Workers experience higher levels of stress, frustration, mental effort, feeling of time pressure and mental workload when switching tasks.

For many people it is important to quickly respond to things that feel urgent. If you start your day like many people by checking your email and Facebook, there will be numerous messages for you to respond to, creating a sense of urgency. If you let yourself be pulled into other people's demand for action, you immediately turn over control of your day to external control. This can have you playing cognitive catch-up all day. Even if you check email and don't respond until later, you may experience a lack of focus because you know you will have to address a certain message later in the day. I found that when I see a newspaper in the morning, my brain immediately goes to work trying to solve the problem behind what ever piece of bad news is featured that day: hunger, war, homelessness, etc, when actually, the problems I really need to be solving are the ones that I have set out for in my long-term vision. If a message comes in, decide if it needs your attention immediately; if not, schedule an ideal time to respond.

Should you quit social media?

Social networks are products designed to keep your attention on them. How can we make this as addictive as possible? Be wary of social media if you want to do your best work because it is 'cognitive junk food'. It's very easy to waste time and energy on social media because it's designed to attract your attention away from what you're doing. Be careful about how and when you use social media. Make sure it's not distracting you from achieving your goals.

How do people end up passionate about their work?

Should we buy into the idea of 'do what you love and you will never work a day in your life'? People often come up to me after talks or message me and tell me they are trying to find what they are passionate about so they can make a career out of it. This can create a lot of pressure for people to 'find their passion', if they don't know it already.

It turns out that we are not born knowing our passion. Sometimes it takes years of experimentation with different careers to find one that you are truly passionate about. It is important only to start with something that interests you and allow passion to develop as you gain skills. I've found that improving my skills has led to increased freedom and autonomy to choose what I do to make a living. As a result I have ended up being passionate about what I do.

Training your focus

Leaders are masters at directing attention. First we must master our ability to direct our own attention. Careers across the board improve as we increase our ability for focused attention. In his book *10% Happier*, Dan Harris says that meditation is like focused reps for your mind (Harris, 2014). We can extend the analogy back to sports again and think of focus like a muscle. If you aren't used to focused and concentrated effort on your work, it will feel really hard (that is what being out of shape feels like). The good news is that it doesn't take long to get back into shape. Meditation is a great companion to focus work because it allows us to reduce our reactivity to small distractions. Meditation also helps you understand how your mind works and reacts – which is important when you get to the most challenging moments of deep work and feel like bailing. You can apply the problems-solving meditation in Chapter 3 to your meaningful work problems.

If your brain has been trained to get novel stimulus at every turn through social media and the internet, then you will have a much harder time concentrating on your work. I use the time I have with my baby son to train my ability to concentrate. It became very apparent to me that I had gotten out of shape in my ability to focus – every 20 minutes or so while we are playing, I am tempted to check my phone, or go and do something else (and sometimes I do check my phone). But I know if I can stay present with him while we are playing, then I will be able to focus more on my work the next time I have a long and challenging task.

Intention

When you sit down at your desk to spend some time doing focused work, take a moment to set an intention around your effort. What is the outcome you would like to achieve and what is your time limit? Maybe it's 'I need 30 minutes to draft a newsletter'. Ask yourself: 'who do I need to be in order to get this accomplished?' Let your actions flow from being the best version of yourself. Connect back with your why. Why is this specific action necessary for my overall vision? Who needs me to show up as my best for this activity?

Flow states

Doing our best work often comes with solid goals, deadlines, feedback and challenges. This is the perfect atmosphere to move us into a state of optimal experience or what Mihaly Csikszentmihalyi calls 'flow' in his book *Creativity: Flow and the discovery of invention* (Csikszentmihalyi, 1996). Steven Kotler, founder of the flow genome project which trains people how to get into this advanced state of concentration, calculated that a challenge has to be 4 per cent harder than your current skill level to find the quickest access into flow states (Kotler, 2014). So getting into a flow state is easiest if you are stretching slightly beyond what you are currently capable of doing.

To do your best work you also want to set stretch goals that force you to be productive. With a hard deadline, you are more likely to step up to the challenge. This is where having a mentor or coach can come in handy. It is harder for us to see what we are capable of, so try goal setting in conjunction with another person.

When designing your career, make sure you pick something that will continue to provide opportunities to be challenged FOREVER. The worst job I ever had was being a microbiologist, because I mastered most of the tests within weeks and was regularly bored. When I reinvented my career as an adventurer, coach, author and podcaster, I chose things where I expected to find challenge for decades.

Cognitive misers

You may have had the experience of eating right all day – choosing vegetables and whole foods over salty snack and junk food. But then all of a sudden, late at night you find yourself drawn to the chocolate biscuits and before you know it, you have consumed the entire bag. This happens because you have burned through your will power and decision-making ability from the countless decisions, big or small, you have made throughout the day.

When Barack Obama was president, he was well aware of the need to conserve his willpower for big global decisions. Obama would put on the same colour suit each morning, do the same workout routine, and have the same breakfast, so that the first decision he made each day was an important one. 'You'll see I wear only gray or blue suits,' Obama says. 'I'm trying to pare down decisions. I don't want to make decisions about what I'm eating or wearing. Because I have too many other decisions to make' (Lewis, 2012).

Knowing this, I have asked my partner Heidi not to ask me what I want to eat for dinner that night, so only one of us has to think hard about that process. When you ask other people to make a decision, you are depleting them of key willpower. I always recommend making suggestions (for restaurants, activities, etc) to your group instead of asking everyone what they want to do. The added benefit is that you come across as a leader with a plan.

Showing up

Sometimes with knowledge workers, there is a tendency to procrastinate. On the other hand, something similar to 'writer's block' does not exist among blue-collar jobs. The cashier behind the counter or car mechanic doesn't get to decide when they are going to serve customers or not. Even if your aim is to do deep work, if you make it your job to just show up and do the work for a certain number of hours, the law of large numbers means that you increase the odds of creating prolific quality output.

Swing for the fences

If you have to choose between doing more work and doing better work, chose better work. Look at Harper Lee, author of *To Kill a Mockingbird* – for decades, that was her only book, yet she is regarded as one of the greatest American authors. Derek Muller from the YouTube channel Veritasium told me that it is better to swing for the fences and produce a single video that might go viral instead of producing daily videos and hoping all the views will add up. For an entrepreneur, this might mean doing three to five major launches in a year instead of ten or more. This means doing your research to find out if there is a demand for your video or product or widget, and having conversations with real people. This means getting lots of feedback and input and beta testers. For a YouTube video this might mean you invest in high production quality, good camera and microphone, skilled camera operators, write a script instead of winging it, and create a professionally edited output.

Collaboration

In the book, *Think and Grow Rich*, Napoleon introduces the idea of the mastermind, a group of like-minded individuals that get together and learn and push each other (Hill, 1937). We can harness the power of our peers when it comes to doing our best work. When you surround yourself with high performers, you automatically generate social pressure of keeping up. This is why you should aim to be the dumbest person in the room, at least part of the time.

Interacting with people leads to the generation of new ideas and motivation. However, this has mistakenly led to the popularization of open office floor plans, which are meant to encourage spontaneous encounters. Cal Newport proposes a better model that will allow for these cross-disciplinary interactions while still creating space for focused concentration – the hub and spoke model. Having a centralized space that allows people to cross paths when they leave their sanctuary of focus (private office) allows people to choose when they are focusing and when they are sharing ideas (Newport, 2016). When I have lived in houses with other entrepreneurs, the dinner table was often the centre of collaboration. How can you arrange your work surroundings to establish privacy and interaction?

Saying no

Once you have figured out what the most important productive outcomes of your career, year, and day are, then you may need to start eliminating things on your to do list. Derek Sivers says that at the beginning of your career, you should be saying yes to almost every opportunity, because you never know where the golden opportunities might come from (Sivers, 2015). But once you are more established in your career journey, you will be getting too many opportunities to handle, and you will need to turn down or pass on many of those opportunities. It's a great practice to pass on opportunities to people who are more able and interested in them than you. For example, if you have all the clients you can handle, send clients to your peers that need them.

Likewise, if there are things you can completely eliminate from your schedule, because they don't align with your mission, then that will free up your time for more valuable work.

Delegate

To be able to delegate, you need to know what your most valuable activities are. Is it making sales, or crunching numbers on a spreadsheet? Is it giving presentations, or writing blog posts? Knowing which of your activities are high leverage (bring in the most important results) can help you decide what to delegate.

Having a good team in place means you can delegate activities to competent people who can do them at least as well as you. This is something that many people have trouble with, because we think nobody can do our work as well as we can. A good rule of thumb is if somebody can do something 70 per cent as good as you, it is time to turn over responsibility for those less important tasks.

Invest now in saving your time later

Just like you invest money, if you can create systems for yourself that by creating them will save you time over the long term, ie spend 20 hours this month on something that will save you 100 hours this year overall, you are getting back more time, which is rarer and more valuable than money.

Ways to invest in your time

There are many simple ways to save you lots of time by investing in tools and services that will streamline your work. The tools that I use to invest in my time are:

- *Automated scheduling tools* – to eliminate back and forth emailing to schedule appointments.

- *Social media automation apps* – so that things like messaging new followers happen automatically.

- *Virtual assistant services* – using skilled remote workers to take over specific time-intensive tasks.

- *Fast listening speed on podcasts and audiobooks* – get to the important stuff faster, and slow down to normal speed if you need to.

- *Email templates for emails you send repeatedly* – when I am inviting people to events, or reaching out to potential clients, the majority of my message (the details) will be similar and I can use the same template over and over with some added personalization at the beginning.

- *Creating standard operating procedures (SOPs) for your team* – these are step-by-step procedures for accomplishing a common task (how to edit an audio/have a sales conversation/write a report) that allows anyone on your team to generate the same result and make the same decision without having to ask for help.

- *Learning keyboard commands for your computer* – in our interview Fabian Dittrich told me that he was able to go from an eight-hour workday to a three-hour workday while taking his company on the road in South America, largely by learning the most effective keyboard shortcuts for his data migration work.

- *Email auto responders and dedicated emailing times* – don't take on other people's urgency! You can set email response expectations with an auto responder and batch your emails so that you do them all at once in chunks once or twice per day (morning and afternoon).

Find out from people doing well in your industry what tools they use to improve their productivity and free time to focus on their best work.

Conclusion

In this chapter you have learnt why it's so important to focus on doing your best work by prioritizing what's going to give you the best outcomes. You have understood the benefits of using your schedule to be more productive by rethinking your morning routine and managing your energy. Finally you have identified ways to avoid distractions, delegate tasks, invest in your time and be more productive in your work life.

Focusing your energy on doing your best work will free up time to learn new skills important to reaching your potential, which we will cover in Chapter 5.

Works cited

Burchard, B (2017) *High Performance Habits: How extraordinary people become that way*, Hay House

Csikszentmihalyi, M (1996) *Creativity: Flow and the psychology of discovery and invention*, Harper Perennial

Currey, M (2013) *Daily Rituals: How artists work*, Knopf

Duckworth, A (2016) *Grit*, Collins

Elrod, H (2012) *The Miracle Morning: The not-so-obvious secret guaranteed to transform your life (before 8AM)*, Hal Elrod

Fallon, N (2017, 11 July). *What's Your Most Productive Work Time? How to Find Out*. Retrieved 25 February 2018, from Business News daily: www.businessnewsdaily.com/8331-most-productive-work-time.html

Goleman, D (2013) *Focus: The hidden driver of excellence*, Harper

Harris, D (2014) *10% Happier: How I tamed the voice in my head, reduced stress without losing my edge, and found self-help that actually works*, It Books

Hill, N (1937) *Think and Grow Rich*, General Press

Kotler, S (2014) *The Rise of Superman: Decoding the science of ultimate human performance*, New Harvest

Lewis, M (2012, October) *Obama's Way*. Retrieved 19 February 2018, from *Vanity Fair*: www.vanityfair.com/news/2012/10/michael-lewis-profile-barack-obama

Newport, C (2016) *Deep Work: Rules for focused success in a distracted world*, Grand Central Publishing

Pattison, K (2008, 28 July) *Worker, Interrupted: The cost of task switching*. Retrieved 19 February 2018, from Fast Company: www.fastcompany.com/944128/worker-interrupted-cost-task-switching

Sivers, D (2015) Derek Sivers on Developing Confidence, Finding Happiness, and Saying 'No' to Millions (T. Ferriss, Interviewer)

Thibodeaux, W (2017, 27 January) *Why Working in 90-Minute Intervals Is Powerful for Your Body and Job, According to Science*. Retrieved 25 February 2018, from INC: www.inc.com/wanda-thibodeaux/why-working-in-90-minute-intervals-is-powerful-for-your-body-and-job-according-t.html

Weinschenk, S (2012, 18 September) *The True Cost Of Multi-Tasking*. Retrieved 25 February 2018, from *Psychology Today*: www.psychology-today.com/blog/brain-wise/201209/the-true-cost-multi-tasking

05
Accelerate your learning

Our ability to quickly learn complex skills, use new computer programs, become comfortable in new environments, build a base of knowledge to access creativity, understand cutting-edge ideas, identify patterns and continue the progression of our learning and understanding, is one of the best ways to stay valuable in a changing workforce. The methods of repetitive study and rereading that many of us learned in school are simply too clunky and inefficient to progress through large chunks of information quickly.

In this chapter we will examine many of the tools and techniques that the world's super learners, memory champions and top performers use to stay at the top of their game. We will hear about Jonathan Levi, creator of the popular Udemy course SuperLearners, entrepreneur Derek Sivers, and learning hacker Scott Young. In our interview, Levi told me that the biggest resistance people are likely to experience when they think about learning, is the massive amount of new information that is being generated in every field. However, that feeling of being overwhelmed by the sheer volume of information can be combatted with the right tools.

There are two types of learning outcomes: skills that you need right now to help you achieve your goals, and future knowledge that forms your frameworks of thinking and will be useful down the road. I often assimilate both types of learning outcomes each day – I will read about copywriting and then implement what I have learned immediately when sending out an email newsletter. I may also read about economics or history, simply to broaden my basic understanding and use as a foundation for linking new ideas later on.

In this chapter, we will get into the specifics of how to use our natural biology and neurology to learn more quickly, covering things such as how to speed read, how to remember people's names, and how to retain and recall complex bits of information. We will also learn how to approach learning a new skill: how to think about practice, finding mentors, understanding where to place your efforts and how to save time.

Once you master the art of accelerated learning, you arrive at a place where you are able to play, experiment and generate brand new knowledge.

How I approached learning sales as a skill

Let's start with a story about learning. Last year, I wanted to really grow my business, and after reflection during my annual review process, I realized that sales skill was the number one thing that would enable me to achieve that growth.

I approached the process in a similar way to when I was a cyclist and wanted to learn how to race a specific discipline or in grad school when I wanted to learn how to cultivate hard-to-grow extremophiles. I knew that sales skill was not something that could be acquired in just a few days, so I prepared for it to be a months- to years-long effort. The first thing I did was start listening to sales podcasts and buy a few of the top sales books on Amazon. Then I started recording my sales conversations and going back and listening to them. Then I approached Emily Utter, a sales coach who had appeared as a guest on The Art of Adventure, and hired her. I followed her seven-part course on sales, created specifically for coaches like me. I listened to each of these training modules several times, including while I was out walking or cycling. I even went to a time share sales pitch (well known for being a high-pressure sales situation) in Mexico and took notes on their sales process.

Once I understood the concepts, I would rehearse before each sales conversation. Sometimes I would role play the conversations with peer coaches. When I encountered new situations in the sales conversation that I didn't know how to handle, I would go back to my coach for advice. Often the differences were minor tweaks to the questions I was asking, levels of enthusiasm, or how I was leading the conversation. I used to cycle more than 10,000 miles per year, and I made sales conversations my new miles. I set a goal of 100 sales conversations. After each call, I would rate myself with how well I implemented my training and record the notes in a logbook. I set automated reminders to follow up with people when conversations were incomplete.

The result? I grew my business by 300 per cent in just eight months, including making $41,000 in a week, and filled my coaching practice. Of course I have off days like any athlete and I have days where all my training pays off and I have a near flawless performance. In addition to this sales skill, there were plenty of other skills I was learning concurrently – how to build and manage a team, how to lead business/adventure retreat effectively, and how to leverage Instagram, to name a few.

In fact, I was using a number of different techniques in this example: deliberate practice and progressive mastery, immersion, deconstruction, spaced repetition and mentorship. We will go in detail through these techniques in this chapter.

Have a reason for learning

Before I lived in Spain and Mexico, I had such a hard time learning Spanish. But once I was using only Spanish daily, I had a great incentive to learn the language quickly. Make sure you are sure why you are trying to learn a particular skill or body of information in the first place. You can take it a step further to trying to solve a problem before you have the skills to solve it. This will frame the context of your learning – in exactly what situation will you be using your new knowledge? Get curious – it is easier to learn things that we feel pulled to learn more about.

Deliberate practice

'The most important gifts we can give our children are confidence in their ability to remake themselves again and again and the tools with which to do that job,' writes Anders Ericsson in his book *Peak*.

Ericsson refers to the term 'deliberate practice' as mastery of successively more difficult specific skills (Ericsson, 2016). Later in this chapter we will look at a step-by-step process. The skills are ones that will lead to success in real-world practice. Ericsson notes that basic ability is important at the start of learning a new skill, but at higher levels it all comes down to training. The same is true for you – only training will get you to the higher levels of competency. The goal is to move a skill from conscious competence to unconscious competence. What this means is that with training, you will no longer have to think about how you perform a skill in order to do it well.

What happens with most people when they approach learning a skill is that they practise enough to get to a level of competence that they find acceptable, and then stop progressing. Even though they might continue to engage in an activity (like driving a car) for decades, they stop progressing. So if you have determined that a particular skill will make you more valuable in your career, you can choose to move past the point of acceptable and into the realm of world class. To continue your progress, you will need a good reason to put in more effort, expert feedback on your current skill level, and an understanding of what world-class skills look like, and ways to practise and acquire better skills.

Deliberate practice is valuable in two ways. You can use deliberate practice to progress faster than most other people, or you can use the process to achieve a more sophisticated level of mastery. Let's start with a method for understanding any skill, and then how we can apply what we know to our training.

Embrace the struggle

It is important to remember that accelerated learning will make you uncomfortable. When you are doing something that pushes you past your current abilities, you will be reforming the neurons in your brain, making new connections – the beauty of neuroplasticity. The actual feeling of this might even be painful, in part because you are changing the homeostasis of your body. In *The War of Art*, author Stephen Pressfield calls this feeling 'The Resistance', and suggests we use its presence as a sign that we are working on something meaningful (Pressfield, 2003). If you can learn to associate this type of discomfort with the excitement of progressing in your skill of choice, you shift to a place where you welcome the discomfort. Across the board, no one feels at ease during challenging practice, but they do love the improvements it brings in their skill.

Deconstruction

Before we go deeper into understanding deliberate practice, let's learn how to deconstruct a skill we would like to learn. This will allow us to determine what the significant elements of a skill are before we start training. Author Tim Ferriss features a learning formula that starts with deconstruction in his book *The Four-Hour Chef* (Ferriss, 2012). The formula is 'DiSSS: Deconstruct, Selection, Sequence, and Stakes'.

In the *deconstruction* phase, the idea is to understand all the single unit building blocks of individual skills that make up a complex skill. 'What are the minimal learnable units, the LEGO blocks, I should be starting with?' asks Ferris. This is where your mind mapping will come in handy to see all the elements laid out in front of you. Start with what you know about your target skill and the order that you expect to learn them in. Then seek out an expert or coach to fill in your blind spots.

Selection is where you determine what are the most effective building blocks. Here we will use Pareto's principle, known as the 80/20 rule, which says that 80 per cent of your results will come from 20 per cent of your efforts. You might be able to guess some of the more important building blocks, and you can also gain a lot of insight into which skills are important to start with by doing interviews with experts and mentors. When I interview someone on the Art of Adventure, I often ask: 'What would you do next if you were running my business?' When talking to an expert, it can be helpful to ask about cases where people have progressed rapidly. They might be starting with different building blocks than traditional progression. Just because something has always been done a certain way doesn't mean it is the best progression for you.

Sequence is where you decide what order you need to learn the building blocks.

Stakes are the consequences – coming back to why.   Often it can be helpful to have both a stick and a carrot – a reward for succeeding and a punishment for failure. In Chapter 10 I'll tell you about a game I played with my partner Heidi – the stakes were that the winner had to buy the loser a massage – both a carrot (massage) and stick (paying for the massage).

Topic immersion

During your efforts at deconstructing, it is helpful to immerse yourself in a topic. I didn't truly understand virology until I started writing my master's thesis after several years in grad school. It was only after reading hundreds of scientific papers that I was able to begin to see the complete picture of the field and place the relevance of my own work. A better approach might have been to start my graduate programme with the immersion that I eventually did for my thesis. Similarly, I was prepared to launch my own podcast after listening to hundreds of podcasts on my daily commute.

When I was immersed in learning chess in college, a funny thing happened. I would walk across the campus and start to see people as chess pieces, like the life-size chess scene in *Harry Potter*. That is when I knew I was truly learning to think like a chess player.

Find the top podcasts, books, blogs, magazines, YouTube channels and social media influencers about your skill of interest and take a deep dive into the material. I've used this technique recently to immerse myself in the worlds of Instagram marketing, Airbnb rental property and running business retreats. It works like a funnel in the sense that it starts with a great input of information, of which, at the start, you don't know which element will be the most significant.

Jonathan Levi told me about the immersive habit he sees in successful people: 'Every brilliant idea in the world of business, in nonprofits, and government comes in the form of an answer to a problem. If you're not reading, you don't have access to the important problems, and the solutions we should be developing.' By ensuring we immerse ourselves in reading about our subject, we become aware of the blank space on the map, where no one has created the needed solutions yet. If you have ever thought, 'What can I do? All the interesting problems have been solved already,' then immersion is your chance to find your own interesting problem to work on.

Immersive tool: speed reading

Once you have decided on the subject you would like to immerse yourself in, there are a couple of ways of speeding up the process. Speed reading isn't just about reading faster, it's about understanding and remembering what you read. It is easy to double or triple your rate of reading and increase comprehension of key information at the same time. Here are some of the most effective components of speed reading:

- *Only read the big words.* The big words are the meaningful ones. Look at the nearest piece of writing to you. You will see that Of, And, Are and The, along with the rest of the two and three letter words, take up half the space on the page! Skip those and you only have to read half the words, doubling your rate. You will still get the important information.

- *Block the lines above the line you are reading.* We waste a lot of time going back and re-reading the previous sentence to make sure we understand. Don't worry – your brain will get it, even if you are worried that you won't remember. Feel free to prove this to yourself by having someone quiz you about what you read. I use a note card and move down the page as I read.

- *Don't speak the words in your mind.* We can talk about 250 words/minute, but our brain can think about 400 words per minute (Institute, 2001). If you read at the speed you would talk, that gives your brain 150 words per minute worth of time to wander, which can make you distracted. The faster you go, the less you daydream, the more you remember. There is no way to fully eliminate your mind wandering, just reduce the occurrence.

- *Eliminate distractions.* Turn off your phone's ringer, the TV and get to a quiet place where you can concentrate. Researchers that have studied multi-tasking have proven decreased performance across all tasks as a result of reduced focus (Bradberry, 2014).

- *Only read what is worth reading.* This goes against what we were taught in school. You don't have to read the book cover to cover! Only read the parts that are worth something to you. The same goes for magazines and blogs. If the book turns out to not be interesting or worthwhile, you can stop reading.

- *Know what you want to get out of reading.* We pay more attention to things that are applicable to us. This relates to the point above, and allows you to have a conversation with the author about what is important for you. Additionally, if you are looking for some specific bit of information (such as a certain name), you can often scan quickly and find it. Remember that if you only need to get the gist of something, that will speed you up; if you have to memorize something, that will slow you down.

Try this too: speed listening

My good friend Ladan Jiracek of the Travel Wisdom podcast is subscribed to nearly 120 other podcasts and has gradually trained himself to listen at speeds of 3.7 times the normal speaking speed using a podcast app such as Overcast. The trick is to gradually increase the listening speed so you get used to the sounds. Speed listening can also be used with audio books. Just like in autoracing or speed reading, you can train your comfort with speed. I recommend using this only when you want to get a broad overview of new topics or to quickly review ideas that you have encountered already. You can also speed up how fast you watch videos with the Enounce software.

Mentors

Finding a mentor is one of the first steps in starting a learning journey – think Luke Skywalker finding Obi Wan in *Star Wars*. Tony Robbins often says the fastest way to learn is to model someone who has done exactly what you want to do. This is because there are patterns to consistent outcomes – luckily, our brain is a pattern recognition machine.

In combination with immersion, mentors can point you where to look for selection and sequence of learning, and what major mistakes you can avoid. The best mentors are people who have already been actively involved in your field of interest. Look for people who have a bias towards action rather than philosophy, because they will have gotten more mistakes out of the way. Your path will be easier if you find a mentor who is motivated to share his or her knowledge and contribute to the next generation's (and your) success.

Linda Rottenberg, who has been called a 'mentor capitalist,' told me that one of the best ways to look at mentorship was a 360-degree experience. You should have some people that are older and younger than you, people that are inside and outside of your industry. Rottenberg says, 'Frenemies sometimes make some of the best mentors, as with Steve Jobs and Larry Page and Sergey Brin.'

I often advise clients to build a personal advisory board in the course of their strategic relationship building so as to get a handful of mentors in place before you think you need them. And don't worry – these relationships only need to last as long as they are valuable. When I was a cycling coach (who worked largely with beginners), I would tell my athletes: when you get to be a professional, it is time to seek out the next level of coach to keep progressing.

Ask for discreet advice from your mentor. If you want to start a mentorship relationship, the worst thing you can do is write an email that amounts to, 'Hey really busy person, can you coach me for free for some unnamed length of time?' A much better way to go about it is to first do everything you can to answer your questions using what they have already written and put out in the world. Think about how they might approach your problem. Finally, if you are really stuck, you can reach out and say something like: 'You wrote in your book that we should try XYZ, but I wasn't able to get that to work. Here are some ways that I think I might solve the problem, Should I do option 1, 2 or 3?'

In his book *Mastery*, Robert Green talks about the apprenticeship phase of mastery. Green's phases of mastery include observation (passive mode), skill acquisition (practice mode) and experimentation (the active mode). Part of the idea here is to place yourself in work situations where you will be acquiring the skills you need to move forward. Always be looking ahead to the next level of your career and think about what skills you might need. Then, take on roles and projects where you can learn the building block skills. This is 'mentorship by situation'.

Getting good feedback

One way that a mentor can help you is through feedback and constructive criticism. In a field like music or gymnastics that has been around for centuries, people have become progressively better and pushed the limits of what is possible. This partly comes from the accumulated knowledge for better methods of teaching those skills.

An outside mentor or coach can see a bigger picture that you can't. As a cycling coach, I designed daily workouts designed to match and slightly exceed the athlete's current skill level. If we did the same workout two weeks later, the body would have adapted and the workout would be too easy and progress would begin to slow down. Having an expert teacher means you can design your practice efforts to match your skill level and progression.

Progressive mastery

Now let's go back to Ericsson's idea of deliberate practice. How you spend your time practising is important. The scale or quality of practice can go from messing around, to unguided regular practice, to deliberate practice, to progressive mastery. In his book *High Performance Habits*, Brendon Burchard lays out the steps for his concept of 'progressive mastery'.

The steps to progressive mastery:

- *Determine a skill you want to master.* Let's work with an example – say you want to get better at sales because you know that will grow your business the fastest.

- *Set specific stretch goals.* You decide to have 30 sales conversations this month.

- *Attach high levels of emotion and meaning to the process and outcome.* You need the money from sales to hire your brother to help you.

- *Identify factors critical to success (through deconstruction and interviews).* You determine that a critical factor is your ability to showcase the value of your offer during the sales conversation.

- *Develop visualizations that allow you to understand what success (or failure) looks like.* You run through your sales script in your mind before each conversation.

- *Schedule challenging practice sessions developed by experts.* You hire a sales trainer and role play with a buddy who is also working on sales.

- *Measure your progress and get feedback.* Your buddy gives you feedback and your trainer makes suggestions based on that feedback.

- *Practise and compete with others.* You track your percentage sales conversion and compare it with your sales buddy.

- *Continue challenging yourself with harder and harder goals.* You raise your rates and approach high-level customers once you have some successful deals go through.

- *Teach what you have learned.* You organize a sales group in your business to train your team based on your experience from 30 sales conversations.

In my experience learning dozens of different sports, languages, business and academic subjects, I have found a few of these steps to be the most important: good coaching and feedback along with clearly defined and challenging goals. The rest fall into place once you get these handled.

As you will see in Chapter 10, if you can frame your thinking in areas where there is no direct challenge (such as being a business manager or gardener) in such a way that you are challenging yourself, then you are more likely to stay engaged in the difficult parts of skill acquisition.

An MIT computer science degree in one year

I was really excited to bring Scott Young on the Art of Adventure because he was the first person to complete the full MIT computer science degree (normally four years), using remote learning, in just a single year. Scott was the first person to attempt doing a full degree at an accelerated pace. 'My goal for this project was to see if it would be possible to push the expectations for how long, how costly and how conventionally an education must be obtained,' says Scott.

Derek Sivers tells the story of his performing arts university instructor who told him, 'normal speed is for chumps'. Most universities cater to the average speed of learning. But if you are highly motivated and focused, you don't need to go that slow. In *Superconductors*, we are placing a priority on being able to acquire new skills in a changing workplace, so we want to set our sights on what the top performers' learning rates are.

What enabled Scott to finish the curriculum so much faster than normal? He combined focus (as in Chapter 4), learning techniques such as spaced repetition, testing, and a good reason – to establish a new baseline for online learning. Because each course built upon the previous one, cramming (short-term memorizing) was not an option. Scott was able to devote more of his attention to the coursework than a normal MIT student, who would likely have additional extracurricular activities placing demands on their time.

Learning and biology

When you are learning new skills, you want to take advantage of our biology to enhance learning. Memory lives in the neurons of your brain, so let's think like a biologist and understand how we can maximize the hand we have been dealt.

Jonathan Levi taught me how to think about the efficiency of the brain: 'Your brain is extremely effective in getting rid of useless stuff because there is a maintenance cost to every bit of information.

Twenty per cent of the energy in your body goes into supporting the brain, and so the more efficient it can get in using energy the better for survival.'

Memory palaces

How did ancient humans remember such extensive oral histories before there was writing or computers? Let's go back to human's earliest memory technique: the memory palace. This is the same technique that modern-day memory champions like those featured in Joshua Foer's book *Moonwalking with Einstein* use to memorize the random order of decks of cards in minutes or Pi to 35,000 digits (Foer, 2011).

The premise is that the learner can remember any number of things by imagining a walk through a real place, such as a palace with many rooms. When I was first learning this technique, I started with a place that was familiar to me – the house I grew up in. In each room you will encounter a scene that triggers the memory you stored there, the weirder and more vivid, the better. Why does this work?

Jonathan Levi explains that, 'We need visual markers to remember anything effectively. There is a hierarchy of memorability of the senses, smell and taste being the most memorable senses. You'll never forget your first love's perfume – you might smell it 25 years from now it will instantly take you back. Unfortunately, you can't remember a book by smelling it unless you're reading a cookbook with all the ingredients alongside. You can't really smell your way through knowledge.' So memory palaces try to cram as many different sensory markers into a scene and link that scene with the thing you are trying to remember – whether it is a deck of cards or a public speech.

We can see the relics of ancient memory palaces today. Levi told me, 'If you look at the *Odyssey*, or the *Iliad*, these multi-thousand-year-old works, you see that they repeat on themselves. Researchers have come to the decision that they were set in a memory palace for a thousand years or so, and somewhere along the way were put to paper. The reason the story returns on itself, the reason it is told the way it is, was because it was stored in a memory palace.'

The importance of recall

The harder it is for you to recall new learning from memory, the greater the benefit of doing so. It will feel easier to simply re-read the text of new material you are studying, because you are already familiar, but this is a trap. This is why the end-of-chapter tests in university textbooks are so valuable. If you are unable to recall the information, you can then go back to the original source material and learn it again.

Likewise, when you teach a skill you have learned, you understand more fully what part challenges people the most. When I was teaching Microbiology at Montana State University, my students were most interested in skills around identifying microbes in the real world. When I worked for 3M, it was my job to train the new interns on all the lab procedures; by the end of my time there I was able to come up with my own new safety measures, as I truly learned where the risks were by teaching.

In Robert Green's levels of apprenticeship from his book *Mastery*, the final phase is experimentation. This is where you progress beyond simply learning skills and use them in new and interesting ways. Let's say you just took a course on presenting at work, you observed some great speakers, and you got some more insight from *Superconductors*. Now you go and prepare your own presentation, using what you have learned, and you add your own special flavour (adding music or robots or puppets, etc) to make it more interesting.

Linking to remember names

In the classic book *How to Win Friends and Influence People*, Dale Carnegie advises us to remember that a person's name is the sweetest sound in any language. So how does Jonathan Levi approach remembering names? He explained it to me in our interview: 'I do something called duel encoding, which means if you tell me your name is Derek I link you to something that's emotionally relevant to me. So, the first thing that comes to mind is I had a friend in college named Derek. So, I've now linked you to him. It just so happens you have the same hair colour as him. So, I've created two linkages. If I met you in a physical space I would mentally store you in that exact area, and then I'd start adding details into that area.'

Remembering names will give you a huge competitive advantage anytime you are building relationships. When you remember someone's name, they know right away that you care about them, and you can build trust more quickly. Many people believe they are simply 'bad with names'. What they are really saying is that they haven't bothered to learn a good technique or placed a priority on remembering names. Imagine you have been at a conference or networking event all weekend. As you say goodbye to the people you have met, you call each of them by name – most people will be blown away and feel a much closer connection to you. Because we all know this is a challenge, we can all appreciate when someone makes the effort to remember us.

Spaced repetition

To acquire long-term permanent knowledge, you need to be able to retrieve what you have learned at some unknown future date. We want to set longer and longer time intervals between when we retrieve this information. Jonathan Levi told me about a software called Anki: 'The software figures out the forgetting curve of your specific brain. We'll determine for each piece of information what your likelihood to remember it is, and then you'll review it three or four times using space repetition, and then you will know it.'

Another approach is to set aside a certain topic that you are learning and move to a different type of learning or topic, and then return to the first. This is called interleaving and eliminates the bias of repeating something over and over, which does not allow knowledge to move into long-term memory.

Sleep: lock in the knowledge

When I was at university, part of my study strategy was making sure I got six hours' sleep every night, even when many of my classmates were pulling all-nighters. Overall, this allowed me to save time studying because I retained the information better. I just had to make sure that I planned my study schedule in advance – I would study one hour each day for a week rather than ten hours compressed right before an exam. According to Jonathan Levi in his Superlearners course, researchers believe that sleep is when we move ideas from our short-term memory into our long-term memory. Sleep also serves the essential function of clearing out toxic metabolic waste from the brain. More active brains generate waste at an increased rate, which explains some of the exhaustion you might experience when you accelerate your learning. You can use a short 15–20 minute nap after an intense session of learning to buffer your short-term memory (Levi, 2016; Rochester, 2013).

Commonplace books

Author Ryan Holiday first introduced me to the idea of commonplace books, which is a physical notebook where quotes, book passages and important thoughts are copied for further reflection and digestion. Commonplace books were popular as a tool until the beginnings of the twentieth century and were used as part of the arsenal of teaching at universities such as Oxford. Milton, Hardy, Emerson and Thoreau all kept their own commonplace books (Holiday, 2014). Many people now use cloud-based document tools such as Evernote and Google Drive, but there is no substitution for keeping a physical notebook with handwritten notes. I like to think of a commonplace book as a cross between a laboratory notebook with observations, a sketchbook, a mind map, journal and an index of ideas.

How can you recreate a commonplace book for yourself? Jeff Brown hosts the Read to Lead podcast, and he told me in our interview about how to engage with a book as you are reading it. I call this reading with intent. You might ask yourself: Do you agree with the author? What is his agenda? What did she leave out that you wish was included? How will this be useful to my own work? Mark Twain wrote in the margins of many of his books, even going as far as to argue with the authors. Pretend everything you read will be material for a book, speech, or later dialogue and record what is significant in your commonplace book.

Derek Sivers' directives

What might come from keeping a commonplace book? In our interview, Derek Sivers said, 'When I'd tell my friends about a great book I'd just read, they didn't want to read it. They didn't want 300 pages of anecdotes, explanations, and supporting arguments. They'd say, "Just tell me what to do."'

Sivers has long published his reading notes on his blog Sivers.org. In preparation for a series of short TED talks, he went through his reading notes again over many months and distilled down the notes even further into single sentence directives – 'Do this or do that.'

These directives represent the accumulation of many processes of distillation. The original book itself is a distillation of the author's knowledge (like this one you are reading). The reading notes are the next level, and the directives are the final level. It takes a lot of work to make sense of an entire book and convert it into a single sentence. Derek said, 'The basic idea of philosophy was to think about our lives and apply practical ways to live better lives. The application of knowledge is a cornerstone of learning. It's the point of learning.'

Visualization and rehearsal

On my birthday in 2006, I won my first bicycle race after retiring from competitive running. I won despite my inexperience, having stiff competition from over 100 riders who were ranked higher than me, and having crashed in a sandy corner with just minutes left to race. How is this possible? I attribute winning largely to mentally visualizing myself winning the race for months leading up to the event.

Studies show it is possible to improve strength without any weight training, simply through visualization. A ground-breaking 2007 study had participants listen to audio that had them imagine they were going through a workout, and the result was nearly the same strength gains (24 vs. 28 per cent) as participants who did physical weight training (Standing, 2007). It is important to visualize in your mind the perfect version of the skill you are trying to learn. I had a ski instructor tell me that the most important ski turns I could make were the last ones of the run before I got on the lift, because those were the ones that I would be replaying while I rode to the top of the mountain. He told me that most people ease off their focus right at the end, and are setting themselves up to rehearse bad form.

This is effective for a physical skill, such as putting a golf ball, or a social skill such as being an engaging conversationalist. Imagery training and visualization is something that lets you overcome your limitations. In your mind you can do something perfectly, even before you are able to in your normal practice.

Let's say you are working on the skill of public speaking, and you want to visualize leading a meeting. When rehearsing a skill, it may help to visualize yourself from a third person vantage, as if in a video game, above your body, You can observe exactly your actions, but also what you are wearing, feeling and how you are moving. You can also observe the room you are in, and the other people in the room and how they are reacting to you. Recreate the experience of really crushing this meeting. If something in your visualization doesn't seem quite right, replay the whole scenario but tweak that part until you get the whole process right.

Chapter summary

In this chapter you have learned how to begin learning a new skill through a process of deconstruction and immersion. You have acquired some tools that allow you to access the right knowledge more quickly, such as mentorship and speed reading. Finally you have understood how the brain works to take advantage of our biology with systems such as spaced repetition, commonplace books and visualization.

I recommend you approach each chapter in this book as its own skill and go through the learning process detailed here for each topic.

You will refine your own learning techniques that suit you the best – such as how I listened to sales training while cycling.

Works cited

Bradberry, T (2014, 8 October) *Multitasking Damages Your Brain And Career, New Studies Suggest.* Retrieved 22 February 2018, from Forbes: www.forbes.com/sites/travisbradberry/2014/10/08/multitasking-damages-your-brain-and-career-new-studies-suggest/#6817438756ee

Ericsson, A (2016) *Peak: Secrets from the new science of expertise*, Eamon Dolan/Houghton Mifflin Harcourt

Ferriss, T (2012) *The Four-Hour Chef*, Amazon

Foer, J (2011) *Moonwalking with Einstein: The art and science of remembering everything*, Penguin Press HC

Holiday, R (2014, 24 January) *How and Why to Keep a 'Commonplace Book'.* Retrieved 22 February 2018, from Ryan Holiday: https://ryanholiday.net/how-and-why-to-keep-a-commonplace-book/

Institute, T P (2001) *10 Days to Faster Reading: Jump-start your reading skills with speed reading*, Grand Central Publishing

Levi, J (2016) *Become a SuperLearner.* Retrieved 22 February 2018, from Udemy: www.udemy.com/superlearning-speed-reading-memory-techniques/learn/v4/content

Pressfield, S (2003) *The War of Art: Break through the blocks & win your inner creative battles*, Warner Books

Rochester, U O (2013, 17 October) *Sleep Drives Metabolite Clearance from the Adult Brain.* Retrieved 22 February 2018, from YouTube: www.youtube.com/watch?v=96aZtk4hVJM

Standing, E M (2007) Mind Over Matter: Mental training increases physical strength, *North American Journal of Psychology*, 189–200

06
Telling your story

A company without a story is usually a company without a strategy.
HOROWITZ, 2014

A friend once asked me for career advice, and so we sat down for a conversation and I asked him, 'What do you do?' After he told me, I had no idea what he was talking about. So I asked him to explain it to me. After he explained it to me, I still had no idea, so I had to try to guess and put it in my own words. You do not want to be like this!

In so many podcast interviews that I do, one of the themes that comes up frequently is how essential it is to be able to talk about what you do. You need to be able to tell your story in such a way that people can understand what you do. You can say it concisely, and leave them asking for more. When you talk about what you do, you need to talk about what your value is without sounding arrogant.

Call it marketing, personal branding or storytelling, you need storytelling skills to sell yourself. Storytelling now plays a major role in business because it helps you explain the value of your product or brand (Wladawsky-Berger, 2017). If people don't understand the value of what you offer then they won't want to buy from you or work with you.

Storytelling is the most effective way of getting an emotional response from your audience, which builds community interaction with your brand and ultimately sells products and services (Howard, 2016). If you can tell a good story about yourself and your business then it's much easier to sell to your audience.

In this chapter we will talk about storytelling as a multifaceted tool: building trust with your audience, capturing attention, making good first impressions, leading your tribe and sharing your value.

According to the *Harvard Business Review*, some of the most popular TV advertisements use the same storytelling structure as Shakespeare – the five act story. Storytelling in advertising evokes strong neurological response in humans – whether it is the stress hormone cortisol during tense moments, or oxytocin from watching cute animals. And people with more oxytocin in their system are more likely to spend money. Stories allow us to focus our listener's mind on a single point of our choosing. Stories connect to our emotions and lead people to take action (Monarth, 2014).

When might a story be useful to your career?

When you go in for a job interview, the best thing you can do is to tell story examples that illustrate your talents and skills that will help you get hired. A story about how you handled a career challenge will illuminate who you are and how you use your skills and abilities. When you are building strategic relationships (Chapter 9), having a collection of breezy, interesting, stories is a useful way of building rapport. When you are attempting to be persuasive and lead your tribe to take action, paint a story for them of an enticing future so they can connect concretely with what it will mean for them. When you want to change the way the consumer experiences a product or service.

Stories make you more relatable; they help you connect with your tribe, and then help galvanize people around your projects and objectives. If you want someone to hire you or fund your company or be your business partner, tell them a story where they can see how they will feel after they work with you.

In his book *All Marketers Are Liars*, Seth Godin says, 'Stories make it easier to understand the world' (Godin, 2005). Stories allow us to experience things we otherwise might never experience (which is why I read so many adventure stories). Stories also prepare us for future situations without having to learn lessons ourselves the hard way. In the same way, you can use stories to help people understand your value before they hire you.

Caroline Weiler is the founder of the Travel Storytelling Festival, and Visual Story Mapping. Incidentally, she was one of the first people to teach me the value of mind mapping (see Chapter 3). I asked her why storytelling was the theme around which all her business projects were centred. She told me, 'Storytelling is important because it's stories that are touching the hearts of people.'

Stories build trust because they help you emotionally connect with your audience. According to Duncan (2014) they are a key part of being a good leader because, by creating an emotional response, stories move people to take action.

In this chapter, I'll show you how to use storytelling to grow your career or business when having a conversation in person, when speaking in front of a group or audience, and online.

Wired for story

Humans are a unique species – we are the only ones who tell stories. We are the species that looked up at the night sky and made constellation from the random assortment of stars and turned those constellations into stories. The medium that we use to tell stories has evolved over the centuries. The earliest recorded stories were simple drawings – it is estimated that the Chauvet cave in France has drawings that date back 30,000 years, and Egyptian hieroglyphics date from 5,000 years ago.

As we learned in Chapter 5, memory palaces were the foundational tools for remembering oral traditions. We use stories to help us make sense of our memories, and our brains are wired for narrative. When I read the books about the Native American tribal traditions, a common theme is telling stories around the campfire at night – tales of bravery from the hunt or the battle. Scholars believe that the *Iliad* is the oldest piece of Greek writing and was recorded from an established oral history. With technology, we have seen a proliferation of storytelling mediums: photography, motion pictures, telephones, radio, TV, digital media, mobile media and social media. Because there is always a human decision maker in charge of hiring, promoting and funding you, let's make the most of stories so we can connect with these people on a human level (Mendoza, 2015).

The stories you tell yourself

If you think more expensive wine is better, then it is.

(Godin, 2005)

To have a supercharged career you also need to make sure that the stories you tell yourself about who you are align with your goals. If the stories you tell yourself support your goals then you'll go much further in your career than if they contradict them. For example, if you believe you are a savvy programmer, then you will have no hesitation attempting to solve a basic coding problem. However, if you tell yourself that you are bad at computers, then there is no way you will even attempt to solve a coding problem. If you consider yourself business minded, good with the opposite sex, articulate, etc, then you are much more likely to take action in entrepreneurship, relationships, speaking, etc.

As my brand, The Art of Adventure, evolved, I had to become more adventurous and live the brand and story I had created for myself. When you find a story that works for you, you need to become that story. For business storyteller, Michael Margolis, story work is both business and personal. In our interview, he told me: 'Learning how to step out of one's story and inhabit a new one is like a new interpretation of the same events. That is the ultimate path of freedom, and that is how you can become, instead of a victim of your story, a master of your own destiny. And that really is the transformational heart of what this story work is all about.'

So you need to choose stories about yourself that will help you be successful and then take the actions needed to make those stories true. In my case I had to become more adventurous so I could live up to the story of my brand. What story about your identity would help you achieve your goals?

Telling a good story in person

Several years ago, I was riding the ski lift with my friend Sam Yount and another random person, and they spent 10 minutes exchanging stories about farming and by the end of the lift ride, the other guy was giving Sam his business card and proposing they do business together.

Sam is now the Chief Marketing Officer for Lending Tree, and I asked him how he tells such good stories. He said the most interesting stories are ones that you have personally experienced. A good story includes lots of detail. Details that have to do with common feelings or easily relatable situations will allow your audience to place themselves in your shoes. Read your audience – if they are into your story, embellish; if not, shorten it. A good storyteller can make a short experience into an hour-long story. Having a collection of good asides to sprinkle in can help extend your tale.

A story tells a person how they should feel about what is happening in the story – often through the eyes of you, the narrator. So when you are constructing a story that you want to use to talk about yourself or your product or project, think about the conclusions that you want your listener to arrive at on their own.

Using stories when doing an interview

In either a media interview or a job interview (or in sales for that matter), you want to be using stories as parable to illustrate your points. Personal stories from your own work life show that you can actually 'walk the talk'. These kinds of stories build credibility and showcase your value as a potential employee, person of influence or expert on a subject.

Tell stories about your successes but don't just boast about what you've achieved. When you are talking about the successes you've had, tell us the story of the problem you faced and how you solved it. Take us behind the scenes of your process so we can see what really happened for you to reach that success.

When you do something well in your work, write it down and use that as a story at your next interview. You can also gather testimonials from people about you or your business and share stories about the impact you created for your clients. Always tell stories that your audience will get. If your interview is for an audience of entrepreneurs travelling with families, then tell a story about how you balance work and family time. If your audience are new entrepreneurs wanting to build a personal brand then tell a story about when you started building your own brand.

EXERCISE – Build your story arsenal

Make a list of at least 10 things that have happened to you that are good stories.

Practise telling these stories with simple narration – a sequence of events. Then start to add elements of storytelling – character voices, changes in pacing and tonality, gestures, etc. Practise telling stories in a variety of different lengths – one minute, five minutes, ten minutes. You might use a shortened version of a story to quickly establish rapport with a new client, a medium length version of a story during a presentation, and a longer version of that story when you are spending time with close colleagues (driving to a trade show).

Elevator pitch

Stories are really important when you're first meeting someone and they ask 'what do you do?' You might have heard of having 'an elevator pitch', which is basically a simple and straightforward way of telling people what you do. We want the elevator pitch to be as succinct as possible. The goal is to generate curiosity and have someone asking to hear more.

The key is to have an interesting story up your sleeve to use once the person you're meeting shows interest in your work. You don't want to launch into a long story straight away because people often ask what you do for work out of politeness and not everyone will be genuinely interested.

I've created a super simple elevator pitch formula you can use over and over in any industry to talk about what you do. The following example uses this formula in a personal conversation you might have at an event:

Person: 'What do you do?'

You: 'You know how people have (fill in the blank problem)? Well I help people (fill in the blank solution).

Person: 'Really? Tell me more!'

You: (Insert interesting story here)

The basic idea here is that you want to generate curiosity with your initial response and then follow up with a longer interesting story that illustrates how you do what you do, or how you go into your area of expertise. The more curiosity you can build with your first answer the better chance you'll have of keeping their attention for your longer story (David, 2014).

When someone asks me to tell them more, I might tell a story about my most recent coaching call where I helped a client plan a speech and use it to build connection with their customers. Or I might tell a story about how one of my clients started a luxury travel company and how a relationship-building strategy helped them get their first customers. I would tailor the example to be helpful to the person I was speaking with. I might also mention what types of opportunities or clients I am looking for: 'I'm always open to talking with high performers that are starting their first online business.'

Public speaking

One of the most common fears is public speaking. And this fear comes from a place where we want to be liked, so we don't become social outcasts. However, your audience is always rooting for you. Public speaking trainer Michael Port told me in our interview that the number one thing to be a good speaker is to serve your audience (Port, 2015). When you tell a good story in service of the audience, they are the ones that benefit.

When we talk about public speaking, I don't necessarily mean you are a motivational speaker – you may also be leading the room at the conference table at work, or giving a toast at your brother's wedding – these are times when you want to be delivering at your best.

Port told me: 'One of the reasons that people get so nervous before a speech is because they want to be liked. They want people to say, 'Yes, you are the best in the world. I've never seen anything like you ever' and they get this idea that they need to be perfect when they're giving a speech. The paradox of performance is that on one hand, you want to really do a great job. Go out there, do big things, take a risk, and on the other hand, you want to go out there and not screw up. Those two intentions are in conflict with each other.'

A good strategy for being liked by your audience is to tell them stories that show your vulnerability. Having read all of Brené Brown's books, I understand the power of being vulnerable to build authentic connection. So I asked Michael Port about how important it was to use stories that showcase vulnerability during a presentation. He said, 'Vulnerability is a tool that you use just like strength is a tool. Just like laughter, love, and playfulness are tools that you'll use when you're giving presentations. Vulnerability has to be used in an honest way. You might allow yourself to be open, and share something that might be a difficult part of our story for them in service of the promise that you've made to them.'

Vulnerability, when used in an authentic way, helps your audience trust what you're saying that they should do to achieve their goals. It shows that you've also been in a difficult place and have found a way out of that.

Contrast while speaking

The perception of expertise often comes from well-organized information.
(Michael Port)

Even the most beautiful note played over and over can get boring, so one of the most important storytelling tools while speaking is the use of contrast. Michael Port (2015) illustrated the three best types of contrast to use while speaking publicly or delivering a performance:

1 *Content contrast.* Contrast within the organization and frameworks that you're using to deliver your content. There are a number of different frameworks. There are numerical frameworks, chronological frameworks, problem-solution frameworks, compare and contrast frameworks, and there are modular frameworks. Then you have more prosaic type content with stories and anecdotes, and these types of content make it a richer experience. A content contrast example would be to start from a numerical framework (here are the five keys to doing x, y and z), and move into a story that highlights one of those, and then move into a problem–solution framework that really breaks down the issues for another one of those keys, and then move into a compare and contrast, etc.

2 *Emotional contrast.* Port cautions, 'If your entire presentation is funny, that's great, but it's just one note. If the whole thing is really intense that's just one note. If the whole thing is really sad that's just depressing.' We are trying to find different emotional courts. So we move from lightness to seriousness to intensity to humour to playfulness, and we keep the audience on the edge of their seat emotionally. If you look at the films that you love that's how you feel. You don't know what you're going to be feeling next, and it's quite an extraordinary feeling to go on that rollercoaster ride.

3 *Delivery contrast.* If you have ever been to a lecture like the many I sat through in grad school, you will know how hard it is to stay awake and engaged in some of them. The professors will often deliver the entire lecture from behind a podium. Often they are using slides and talking about what is on the screen. But lectures, classes, speeches and shows can have plenty of delivery variation. You can create more delivery contrast with video and audio. Michael Port says, 'I use a lot of audio in my keynotes, which is often unique. I even have conversations with other voices coming out of the speakers to play scenes that demonstrate what I'm talking about.'

In addition, try some of these elements that I have adapted from the world of acting and improvisational theatre to enhance the contrast of your story. Notice how these are similar to the charisma tools in the next chapter:

- pacing;
- props;

- volume;
- vocal tonality;
- sound effects;
- resonance;
- voices;
- accents;
- emotionality; and
- physical body – posture, gestures, miming.

Storytelling online

Narrative strategist and story-telling expert, Michael Margolis posed an interesting thought to me during our interview: 'Consider this. Before any business meeting you've been Googled.' It means that people are finding a whole bunch of breadcrumbs online that lead them to your 'about me' page. People experience your story before they experience you in real life, and we haven't really been taught or prepared for that new reality, and what is a way of authentically talking about yourself in a way that goes beyond bragging, or apologizing?'

Each new medium for storytelling, from oral histories to the printing press, to social media, changes the way we tell stories. With the rise of the internet, *Wired* magazine tells us that people changed to a more immersive story experience – people want to carve out a role for themselves in your story (Rose, 2011).

My friend Andy Austin is a photographer for *National Geographic* and pioneered the idea of the 'adventure selfie', which is your traditional landscape photo, now with a person in it. When we see a person in a photo, it does two things – it gives the landscape scale, and it allows us to place ourselves in the scene. We become part of the story. With a social media platform such as Instagram, you have both a photo and a caption. The photo sets the mood of the story and the caption allows you to go behind the scenes. How was the photo taken? What were you feeling in the photo? What was the experience like that you are sharing? What were the challenges you faced around making this photo happen? The more you can share behind the scenes of what you are doing, the more interesting your social media will become.

This 'behind the scenes' approach to storytelling can also be used for other social media platforms such as Facebook and Twitter. When you share content you can tell your audience how you feel about it or what it means to you personally.

Your online profiles on your website 'about' page and your LinkedIn profile can also talk about your accomplishments in a way that shares a story about who you are. You can talk about your hobbies or interests and you can tell your readers about why you do your work so they understand what motivates you.

Online storytelling has become more important because it is often the first impression we get of a person.

Common ground storylines

In his book *DotCom Secrets*, digital marketer Russell Brunson introduces the concept of the 'attractive character' (Brunson, 2015). This concept is a way to share your back-story with your audience in a way that helps them identify with you. If you have built a great network of customers or a large email list, but if people are not engaging with you, it could be the relatability of your story. Marketers are always working to build their 'know, like, and trust' factor. The easiest way to do this is in person, shaking hands and having a conversation. But online, we need to share our humanness with our stories.

Here are the six storylines he highlights with my examples of how you could use them:

- Loss and redemption – you lost a close friend and discovered how important relationships are to you. You designed your business around relationship building.

- Before and after – you were a burnt-out corporate slave and now you're happy and fulfilled running your own coaching business.

- Us vs. them – you're someone who values time with your family in contrast to those people who don't get home until their children are already asleep.

- Amazing discovery – you were struggling to achieve your business goals until you discovered a personal insight that radically changed the way you do things.

- Secret telling – you admit to lacking confidence when you first started in your career (sharing some of the things you thought or did while feeling like this).

- Third person testimonial – you taught Katie how to use your formula and her results exceeded expectations. Here is how she made her success happen.

Combine these with the following superhero persona exercise:

EXERCISE – Creating your superhero persona

Here is how to create your own superhero image of yourself and identify your super talents:

Think of your heroes – movie heroes, book characters, rock stars, celebrities, sports heroes.

List their defining traits.

What makes them relatable? Why do we root for them?

What do you like about them?

What is their dark side?

What we see in these heroes are the things we like about ourselves or resonate with who we want to be. Indiana Jones, The Dos Equis 'Most Interesting Man in the World', Richard Feynman and Jimmy Fallon are some of my heroes.

Now that you have created this secret superhero identity for yourself, how does this superhero solve problems? How do they move through life? How do they hold their bodies or speak?

You can use this identity in your 'about' page and bio across all platforms. You can play the role of this superhero when you do your branding and in how you come across publicly.

Tell powerful stories

To get noticed and attract the right audience you need to tell powerful stories. Seth Godin tells us to, 'Make your story bigger and bigger until it's important enough to believe' (Godin, 2005). Even if you think your life isn't that interesting you can make your story more powerful by adding in strong statements of what you believe to be true and important. Not everyone will like you but by making a stand you will be attracting your tribe who will follow you and help you build a successful career.

You can also experiment with different storytelling modes to create powerful stories. I asked Carolyn Elliott about how she has used her PhD in poetry to grow her business so effectively. She told me that 'poetry is the most dangerous type of writing because it doesn't play by the rules'. Poetry allows her to tell her story in a way that is unique, which polarizes readers. Aspire to be powerful and polarizing: vanilla is the worst possible way to go when you tell stories, because it doesn't speak to anyone.

Why? Polarizing stories matter more. To the people that agree and connect with a story, it helps them know that they are exactly who you are speaking to – it galvanizes your tribe around you. To the people who disagree or don't like your story, it is equally valuable because it helps them solidify their opinions and identity.

The chocolate secret

Attracting people to your business can also be achieved by appealing to likes and values most people agree with.

When researching before my interview with Michael Margolis, I saw on his Twitter profile that he loved chocolate. I immediately sent him some chocolate recommendations, because I had recently done a blog post about the best chocolate bars around the world. It was a really easy connection for me to make since I love chocolate, and I asked him about why he mentions chocolate in his Twitter bio given that the bio has to be so short.

Margolis teaches the idea behind the chocolate secret in his business storytelling school. 'Chocolate has become the social lubricant for basically people to say 'me too'!' Bios and about pages aren't about sharing how cool you are or stoking your ego, they are for creating points of engagement. Think about the bridges you can create for your audience to join you in your story.'

Gary Vaynerchuk also uses this marketing strategy in his Twitter profile. Even though he is a well-known entrepreneur and podcaster, his profile reads 'Family 1st! Entrepreneur 2nd'. By showing that his family is important to him, he makes himself more relatable to his audience. Most people who have career ambitions struggle with balancing work and family life so his profile makes his followers think 'me too'.

Like the chocolate example, if you use common interests, values or struggles in your storytelling it will help to build a connection between you and your audience.

Your about page and bio

One of the most clicked pages on any website is the 'about' page. Your social media (such as LinkedIn) bio and about page are a huge opportunity to build rapport with your target audience. So what are some of the important considerations when writing your own or your business's bio?

Michael Margolis told me, 'focus on what we call "who, what, who". So, who you are, what you do, who you serve. You need to establish relevance, and then once you establish relevance, and then you add in a point of view, a unique way that you look at the subject or topic area of work. Then people are going to want to know, "Oh, what's the backstory?" Tell me the superhero origins, like I want to know how did you get into this? What are your influences, what informs this? People will be fascinated with wanting to know the back story, but you need to earn their attention, their respect, and relevance before you can go there. Share what you're most curious about. Share what gives you that fire in your belly.'

Margolis says there is an unconscious question on everyone's mind: 'Are you just trying to sell me more stuff, or do you care about my world and making it better?' So talk about what you care about. Tell them about what you are up to that is in service of something larger than yourself. This is where you take a stand for making the world better for others and share that story. By taking a stand, you invite people into a relationship with you.

Your audience is the hero of your story

As an adventurer, I sometimes fall into the trap of thinking I'll just tell a cool adventure story and people will want to work with me. But it is a mistake to make yourself the hero of your story, or even your brand or product the hero. Make your customer the hero of the story.

Michael Margolis told me: 'At the end of the day we all want stories. Our favourite story is a story that is somehow about us. So, focus on validating your audience instead of validating how cool, special and successful you are, and if you validate your audience's experience where they're like, 'Wow, you really get me. You're really on my side.' If you can talk about their experience exactly, using their words, and truly understand them, people will want to be part of your tribe and become customers if you have the right offer for them.'

Find out what goes on in your customer's head and use those words when you tell a story. Pick something that they will relate to, something that aligns with their worldview, rather than just a good story you want to tell. When they realize that you understand them then they'll want to work with you. As Seth Godin says in *All Marketers Are Liars*, 'you want to remind your audience that they're right' (Godin, 2005).

Conclusion

In this chapter you've learned why it's so important to learn storytelling skills if you want to succeed in your career and business. Telling powerful stories helps your audience see you as relatable, real and trustworthy, which is necessary before you sell them anything.

You've learned how to use stories in interviews, conversations, public speaking and in your online profiles to connect more effectively with potential customers or clients. Now you're armed with techniques and examples that you can start applying in your own work life to create more success for yourself.

In the next chapter we will be enhancing your role as a good storyteller by learning techniques to develop your charisma and confidence.

Works cited

Brunson, R (2015) *DotCom Secrets: The underground playbook for growing your company online*, Morgan James Publishing

David, T (2014, 30 December) *Your Elevator Pitch Needs an Elevator Pitch*. Retrieved 25 February 2018, from *Harvard Business Review*: https://hbr.org/2014/12/your-elevator-pitch-needs-an-elevator-pitch

Duncan, R D (2014) Tap the Power of Storytelling, *Forbes*

Godin, S (2005) *All Marketers Are Liars: The power of telling authentic stories in a low-trust world*, Portfolio

Horowitz, B (2014) *The Hard Thing about Hard Things: Building a business when there are no easy answers*, HarperBusiness

Howard, B (2016) Storytelling: The new strategic imperative of business, *Forbes*

Mendoza, M (2015, 1 May) *The Evolution of Storytelling*. Retrieved 20 February 2018, from Reporter: https://reporter.rit.edu/tech/evolution-storytelling

Monarth, H (2014, 11 March) *The Irresistible Power of Storytelling as a Strategic Business Tool*. Retrieved February 20, 2018, from Harvard Business Review: https://hbr.org/2014/03/the-irresistible-power-of-storytelling-as-a-strategic-business-tool

Port, M (2015) *Steal the Show: From speeches to job interviews to deal-closing pitches, how to guarantee a standing ovation for all the performances in your life*, Houghton Mifflin Harcourt

Rose, F (2011, 8 March) *The Art of Immersion: Why do we tell stories?* Retrieved 25 February 2018, from Wired Magazine: www.wired.com/2011/03/why-do-we-tell-stories/

Wladaswky-Berger, I (2017) The Growing Importance of Storytelling in the Business World, *Wall Street Journal*

07
Portraying your best self

The science of charisma and confidence

Up to 93% of communication can be non-verbal, and your non-verbal signals give 12.5 times more weight to the communication.
VANESSA VAN EDWARDS, *FOUNDER OF THE SCIENCE OF PEOPLE IN OUR INTERVIEW ON THE ART OF VDVENTURE*

There are two ways for other people to see a better version of you. One is to improve ourselves and our skills and hope those speak for themselves. The other is to understand and control how other people perceive us by understanding the science of charisma.

Why developing charisma is an important skill

Imagine two engineers with equally valuable technical skills – both are excellent at what they do. But one of them receives promotion after promotion and positive recognition from his or her peers, while the other struggles to move to more desirable positions or be acknowledged for their work. So what is missing for the second person? Charisma and confidence.

Because you are reading this book, I'll assume you want to open as many doors for yourself as possible. You want to give off the right signals so that people listen to you and take you seriously. You want to be given the opportunities that you deserve. You want to be able to shine and make a difference with the work you do. Master the skills of charisma, confidence and non-verbal communication and you will be well on your way to getting these things.

In this chapter we will define the elements of charisma broadly, and then break down different physical components of body language that influence charisma. We will explore the difference between internal and external charismatic states and the role of confidence in charisma.

When we talk about portraying your best self, we are talking about being authentic. You may be wondering if you will come off as fake if you learn all kinds of charisma-building and body language techniques, but don't feel the same way on the inside. You would be correct: people are able to subconsciously pick up on incongruences between your outer behaviour and how you feel. Think of someone trying to be friendly when they really are in a bad mood – it comes off as disingenuous. We will therefore also address how to create charismatic internal states that match up without charismatic external cues.

What is charisma and who has it?

When I give workshops on charisma, I often start by asking for examples of people who are charismatic. Some names that come up often are: Barack Obama, Will Smith, Oprah Winfrey, Steve Jobs, the Dalai Lama and Tony Robbins. Then I ask – what are the traits that these people have that make them charismatic? Answers include smiling, laughing, confidence, eye contact, good looks, good posture, a strong voice, presence, compassion, nice clothes, and the ability to lead a room. My audience is noticing the outer signs of how a charismatic person looks and acts. People know what charisma is when they see it but we need to break it down so you can recreate it for yourself. In this chapter we will explore the three elements – warmth, power and presence – that make up charisma and how you can add more confidence to your career.

How charisma affects success

When I was a PhD student at Montana State University, I taught the undergraduate Microbiology laboratory course each semester. We had one semester of training before our teaching assignment, but it was by no means a complete training for new instructors. I was teaching 60 students, eight hours a week. Of course, I wanted the best possible outcomes for my students so I made sure I was well prepared with the understanding of the material. But one thing was holding me back – I was a boring teacher and lacked charisma.

I started incorporating stories from my time working as a professional microbiologist to illustrate how we actually used the techniques we were learning in the laboratory. Students seemed to like this, but I knew there was still more I was missing. Besides drawing on skills from my improvisational comedy days at university to be more entertaining, I wanted the students to respect me, pay attention to what I was saying, complete their assignments, and learn as much as possible. I realized that charisma would allow me to better transmit my scientific skills and knowledge.

I did what every good scientist would do in this situation: I started to experiment with ways to portray more signals of competence and charisma to engage my students. I started learning about body language and vocal tonality and different signals that we broadcast. As I implemented the techniques I was learning, I started getting more engaged students: more people were staying after class to ask follow-up questions and more people were participating in the class discussions.

After my first two semesters, I had been given an instructor rating of about 4.5 out of 5. After learning these techniques, the students gave me a rating of 4.98, the highest rating for an instructor that year. Additionally students were scoring higher on quizzes and exams. Since it was the same material each semester, the biggest change was my ability to lead the room. So charisma was improving both my success as an instructor and my students' success in learning.

Elements of charisma

In the book *The Charisma Myth*, Olivia Fox Cabane dispels the idea that people are born with a set amount of charisma. The people who seem to have been born with charisma simply figured it out at a younger age. Steve Jobs is a great example of someone who has continued to improve his charisma throughout his career through deliberate practice, because he wanted to be the best presenter he could be. You can watch the difference by looking up his earlier presentations on YouTube. What a relief! If charisma is a learnable set of skills, it means you can improve your charisma as well. Let's begin with an understanding of what charisma is.

We can break charisma down into three distinct elements:

1 warmth

2 power

3 presence.

Let's illustrate those elements with a story: Imagine that you are a prehistoric tribal hunter gatherer. You are out in the jungle hunting and you encounter a stranger from a different tribe in a clearing. You want to know – is this person a friend or foe? Where is the first place you look? Answer: their hands.

Why? To see if they are holding a weapon.

This process is still part of our wiring today – when you first encounter a new person (like when you pass someone on the street), the first thing that happens is a micro glance at his or her hands (Kohut, 2013). This also explains why you should never stand around with your hands in your pockets, or keep them hidden under a table – subconsciously people will feel uncomfortable because they can't see what you are holding.

After assessing the hands, you then will look up to their face to see if they are smiling and warm with an open posture. So we are assessing this new person for the warmth signals that they are giving off to quickly determine their friendliness. This also indicates that when working on charisma – warmth should be the first thing we work on.

The next thing a prehistoric hunter will want to know is how powerful this person is. Power can be defined as a person's ability to impact their world and make something happen. If this new stranger is friendly and powerful, perhaps they would make a good hunting partner or tribal ally. Does the person appear physically strong, have good posture, move with ease, have a deep commanding voice and hold your gaze? According to *Compelling People*, these relics of our evolutionary history are common indicators of strength that persist to this day.

Warmth and power can dynamically oppose each other if one is prioritized at the expense of the other – think about the American politician Hillary Clinton – she intentionally dialled up her transmission of power at the expense of perception of warmth during the last US presidential election. She wound up with people confident in her ability to lead, but not liking her personally. So be mindful of the situation in which you use warmth or power. For example, if you are a CEO leading a shareholder meeting, power might be more helpful, but if you are a CEO meeting a new supplier, warmth might be more useful.

As we go through different charismatic body language, I'd like you to think about ways you can personally use each of them to increase your warmth or power.

The third and final piece of the puzzle is presence. Presence is a modifier or magnifier of the other two elements of charisma. Harvard researcher Amy Cuddy says: 'Presence stems from believing in and trusting yourself—your real, honest feelings, values, and abilities.' You can interpret this as being authentic. If you want to show power or warmth, you want that to come from a real authentic place inside you – otherwise people will sense the disconnect.

People often know when someone is being present – it feels like you share a little corner of the universe with them– but dialling in your own presence can be a challenge. You also know when someone is not present – think of the last time you had a conversation with someone who was looking at their phone or glancing around the room at an event, looking for someone. The absence of presence can detract from otherwise charismatic behaviours.

Many business people live in their heads, making decisions and understanding facts and figures all day. This can give a faraway impression. It is important to remember that an interaction between two humans is an interaction between two living, breathing and biological organisms. To be present, we need to bring our interaction out of the world of data and information, and into the human-to-human connection. The fastest way to do this is to focus on your own five senses and feelings, and then turn your attention to the person or group of people you are with.

EXERCISE – Get present

Take two minutes and close your eyes and think about these three things:

- Listening: Listen for the sounds in the environment around you.
- Breathing: Feel your breath go in and out.
- Feeling: The sensations in your toes (you can do this anytime you want to feel more present).

EXERCISE – What elements of charisma do you already use?

- What do you *think* about when you're performing at your best?
- How do you *walk* when you're performing at your best?
- How do you *talk* when you're performing at your best?

Body language components

Now we will go through the entire body and understand in detail how the eyes, mouth, voice, posture, touch and internal state affect our charisma.

Eyes

Bill Clinton is one of America's most charismatic leaders. I met him once after a speech and what they say is true – he makes you feel like you are the only one in the room. One of his greatest charisma tools that he uses to establish this presence and connection is his warm eye contact. To copy Bill Clinton, you need a soft and direct gaze. This form of eye contact makes you feel like he really cares about you. A great technique to replicate this is to look at everyone with the caring eyes of a parent. Your eyes need to tell them that you care. In contrast, if you want to have the eye contact of power, think of Clint Eastwood in films such as *Dirty Harry* or *The Good, the Bad and the Ugly*. His eyes are slightly squinted while the rest of his face is relaxed, giving us the 'eyes of steel' look. So you can prioritize a warm gaze for first impression and powerful eye contact for strong leadership, for example.

While it is easy to make eye contact while listening, it is much harder to make eye contact while you are speaking. Holding eye contact while speaking is a signal that you are confident in what you are saying. Psychologist Alan Johnston reports that listeners preferred eye contact for 3.2 seconds (Moyer, 2016). So when you are leading a room, you can move your gaze from person to person through the group every three seconds. One great way to get comfortable holding eye contact is simply to record videos and practise making eye contact with the camera while speaking.

According to Vanessa Van Edwards, in an average one-on-one conversation, the ideal amount of eye contact is 60–70 per cent. If you go above 72 per cent eye contact, it becomes a territorial invasive cue. The good news is that we naturally do 60–70 per cent. But there are a couple of common distractions that can mess you up by decreasing the amount of eye contact: checking your phone, even if you are just looking at the time and looking around at what else is going on in the room.

Kara Ronin made sure to clarify in our interview that in some cultures, such as Japan, a lack of eye contact can be a sign of respect. Make sure you brush up on local cultural cues before you go on a trip, especially if you are going to do business in a new country.

EXERCISE – Eye contact exercise

For strength – make eye contact for three seconds or more at a time when you are talking to someone (it is much easier to make eye contact while listening!). Alternatively, try holding the gaze of someone walking towards you. Do not be the first to look away.

For warmth – when you look at people, imagine that you are someone's parent and that you care about them deeply.

Smile

Research shows that if you put a pen in your mouth and hold it there, you feel happier (Strack, 1988). The theory is that you are tricking your body into thinking you are smiling, putting you in a happier mood. If you ever see me driving, I'm usually smiling like a damn fool to combat getting grumpy from traffic. As the phone sales people say: 'Smile and Dial.' People can even hear when you are smiling over the phone and this signal of warmth makes them more receptive to what you are selling.

Don't worry about forcing a smile, because it will become a natural smile. Smiling gives you a warm internal state. There is an expression coined by Jordan Harbinger to illustrate how our physical body can influence our thoughts and vice versa: 'The mind follows the body and the body follows the mind' (Harbinger, 2015). People like Amy Cuddy and Tony Robbins use their physicality to change their internal states.

EXERCISE – The perfect smile

How do you smile? Mouth open or closed? Toothy grin or closed lips? Head tilted back or forward? Our natural smile might not look the best or appear the most genuine. To train yourself to have the best smile for you, practise as many different smile types on video and take still images of the ones that look the best. Feel free to solicit feedback from colleagues and friends. If you find a different smile that looks better, you may need to practise intentionally until it feels natural. The next step is to practise speaking through a smile. This is especially helpful when you want to transmit warmth and enthusiasm through video or to a room of people. Use your smiling skills anytime you want to emphasize warmth.

Voice

As we learned in the storytelling chapter, there are many elements of the professional actor's trade that we can take and emulate when we want to enhance our charisma. Here, we will break down various aspects of voice that can influence our charisma.

- *Filler words.* Verbal tics and filler words are uncharismatic and distract your listener. You don't want someone focusing on what annoys him or her about your speech patterns when you are speaking. When I started podcasting, I edited my own audio for the first 35 episodes. It was terribly annoying for me to have to hear my own verbal tics. I did lots of lip smacking and 'ums' and 'ahs'. I had to cut each one out of the audio so that the episode would flow smoothly. Faced with such confronting and consistent verbal tics, I made the conscious choice to pay attention when I talked and I have since reduced these substantially.

- *Uptalk.* Some people have a tendency to end their sentences with an upward inflection like they are asking a question, even when they are saying a statement. (I'm Ron Burgundy?) Think about delivering your words like a judge reading a sentence: the verdict is guilty. Uptalk is uncharismatic because it signals that you are not confident in what you are saying. However, you can use rising throughout the entirety of a sentence to create excitement.

- *Volume.* If no one can hear what you are saying, you lose a major signal of power. Clarity is also important – make it easy for people to connect with what you are saying. In group situations, such as a meeting or networking event, most people speak at a level of two or three out of five, but when leading a room, you need to be speaking at a four out of five. Feel free to ask people in the back of the room if you are loud enough.

- *Pacing and the power of a pause.* When speaking, the charismatic speaker knows that he is in control of the room and that no one will talk over him or her. Long pauses build anticipation for the next words. You can also speed up your speaking to build excitement, or slow down to build intensity. I like to over-exaggerate these techniques as if I am reading to a child, because they help people to retain more of what you are saying by interrupting their listening pattern.

- *Resonance.* Deeper and more resonant voices exude more power. Think James Earl Jones as Darth Vader, or Neil Degrasse Tyson. Deepness of voice is a subconscious indicator of physical size and strength. When I wanted to improve vocal resonance, I went to a voice coach who used a drum which she beat next to my lower back. This allowed me to move the location of resonance of my voice to a place that generated a richer, deeper tone. You can think of this as speaking from your hips. Actors and singers use their diaphragm to control the air as it passes their vocal chords.

EXERCISE – Vocal tonality

You can do this while telling a story about your favourite day ever. Practise speaking with a louder than normal voice and make sure you end a sentence with a downward intonation (like you are a judge reading a sentence) and not an uptalk (like in a question?). You can also pause for dramatic effect... mid sentence. You can also whisper to get people to lean in.

Posture

I first encountered power posing from Amy Cuddy's great TED talk and listening to the Jordan Harbinger Show podcast who use the tagline 'the mind follows the body and the body follows the mind', meaning you can influence your internal state with the way you hold your body. Here is a simple prescription – whenever you walk through a doorway, stand tall and smile, because that is when people see you and make their first impression. Other postural signals of confidence include standing with your weight balanced between your two feet, keeping your head level, and pointing your nose at the listener.

Amy Cuddy's research showed that when you take up lots of space – for instance, in the victory pose or the superman pose, your testosterone levels go up and cortisol (the stress hormone) levels go down (Cuddy, 2010). This is a natural human response to feeling good. Conversely, when you take up a small amount of space, you feel worse and testosterone drops. This collapsed body position is exactly the position that hunching over our smartphones puts us in. You can remedy this by holding your phone to the side, which will give you an open body position. Additionally, walking with a bounce in your step and some swagger creates the same boost.

The funny thing about good posture is that it rubs off on other people. In college, my best friend fell out of a tree and broke his back (he is fine now) and had to wear a back brace for six months. We realized that he was actually quite tall but had been slouching the whole time. When we stood in a circle talking, everyone around would stand up straighter like they were all wearing back braces too!

You can enhance someone else's charisma by getting them to open up their posture as well. If your friend is standing with their arms crossed, hand them something, which will force them out of their closed posture.

My pre-podcasting warm-up routine amounts to power posing and smiling for at least two minutes. Then I dance around to a 'pump up' song such as Pharrell's 'Happy' or Macklemore's 'Can't Hold Us'. I close my eyes and think of one of my greatest moments (like the time I won my own Rock Paper Scissors tournament) and also think of the people that love me the most and forgive me even when I'm not perfect. This allows me to tap into my charisma during the interview and feel more confident interviewing important guests.

Hands and touch

My college roommate was going to interview the former vice president Walter Mondale for the school newspaper and was practising his handshake with all of us. His handshake was actually pretty good but we kept telling him it was way too soft ('the dead fish') and so he kept trying to make it firmer and even though it hurt our hands we kept up the joke!

The main benefit of a handshake is that brief skin-to-skin human connection. Hand-shaking or hugging results in a decrease of the stress hormone cortisol, says Matt Hertenstein, an experimental psychologist at DePauw University in Indiana. In addition to reducing our stress response, friendly human touch stimulates oxytocin, a neuropeptide, referred to as the 'love hormone'. Oxytocin lays the foundation for us to feel close to one another (Trudeau, 2010).

When I was a groomsman at my first wedding, the officiant was a military chaplain and told us that instead of standing during the ceremony with our hands behind our backs or in our pockets, just to let them hang casually by our sides. Recall from the story of the hunter at the beginning of the chapter that people will look to your hands.

Hand gestures can help you communicate and connect with your listeners. The most popular TED speakers used hand gestures nearly twice as often as their peers (Gregoire, 2016). As a naturally relaxed individual I don't have massive hand gestures, so when I want to animate my conversation I imagine that I am a highly expressive individual and talk with my hands as well as my words. When you are speaking you can reach out and gesture (with an open hand) to your listener. If they are close enough, you can physically touch them on the arm. Avoid gestures that are too big or cover your face or close down your body language (arms crossed or fingers intertwined).

Create an internal state of charisma

People love people who love themselves.

(Vanessa van Edwards)

We want our external state to match our internal state. This prevents us from coming off as fake. This section will look at getting into a charismatic internal state. Imagine your charisma as 'shining through', like a little sun inside you. Your level of charisma is then transmitted to people through your non-verbal cues, which we have already discussed.

Negativity is a major detractor from charisma. So here we will learn how to bring our focus to the positives and get our thoughts and feelings in positive alignment.

EXERCISE – Self-compassion charismatic internal state

Take five minutes and close your eyes and think about:

- A time (or several) when you did a good deed or helped someone.

- A time (or several) when you were a success or did something really well.

- An all-loving entity past or present, real or mythical like the Buddha, Jesus, Mother Teresa, your mum, or your puppy dog, that has warm affection for you. Feel how much they care about you and forgive you for any mistakes you have made. Feel them completely accepting everything about you.

You have just proven to yourself, based on facts, that you are a good person, a successful person, and you are worthy of love.

Managing your internal state

Did you see the movie about Tony Robbins – *I am not your Guru*? Tony Robbins is legendary for how he can hold an audience of thousands captivated for 12 hours at a time or more. To be able to do this, he needs a strong energy foundation, like we mentioned in Chapter 2. Robbins needs to be able to hold the attention of the person in the furthest reaches of a large arena, so he carefully manages his state. This includes mental, physical and spiritual state.

So how does Tony Robbins achieve such energy and endurance? Before he goes on stage he can be seen bouncing on a portable trampoline called a rebounder. He is moving the lymph around in his body. He also beats his chest and claps his hands together. In the morning he takes a plunge in an ice pool and does breathing meditations. The lymphatic system doesn't have a central pump like the heart, but instead relies on body movement. Lymph fluid is crucial to removing toxins and metabolic waste. If lymph is not flowing properly, people can experience symptoms such as colds and joint pain, and infection. Cold water can help contract tissue and move lymph.

In addition, cold reduces inflammation and releases mood-boosting neurotransmitters (Robbins, 2018; Shevchuk, 2008).

Eliminating barriers to charisma

Imagine you are sitting at a table having a drink with friends at sunset on the beach. The glare from the sun in the water bounces up and makes you squint. Your friend is telling you about their theory that there is a wrinkle in time caused by the large hadron collider. But because you are squinting, your friend thinks you don't believe what she is saying, because you have what appears to be a sceptical look on your face.

Now imagine that it is autumn and you have a job interview. Because it is cold you decide to wear a jumper to the interview. Inside the office however, it's much warmer and your jumper starts to feel warm and itchy. The interviewer notices that you look squirmy and uncomfortable. They wonder if you are uncomfortable because you are trying to hide something.

If you spend a lot of time looking at your smartphone or using a laptop without a stand, chances are, you are hunching over to look at your device, taking up less space, and appearing smaller and weaker. We already know that this can elevate levels of cortisol, but it also detracts from our power signals.

Because other people cannot always accurately decipher the cause of your signals, their meaning is left open to interpretation. But we can do better than that. After reading this chapter and testing some of the ideas, you will be more aware of the signals you give off and, can adjust your environment to ensure you give off the signals you intend to.

Great first impressions

Now that you have mastered some of the different elements of charisma, it's time to go make a great impression on people! So how do you do that?

One thing that is important to remember is that people assimilate a first impression of you the moment they see you. A simple reminder is to always walk through the door with good posture and a smile. Vanessa Van Edwards is body language researcher and founder of the Science of People, and she told me that 'We are 76% accurate in our first impression judge of personality, and people don't usually revise their opinions'. So let's make sure the first impression is a good one!

Vanessa van Edwards had me do an exercise when I interviewed her. She asked me to consider how I wanted to come across when people met me? I replied that I wanted to come across as someone exciting! She told me that one of the number one traits that makes people seem exciting is that they are interested in other people. The science of excitement comes down to dopamine. This is the neurotransmitter that signals reward and pleasure. Dopamine is the chemical explanation for excitement. Do you want to be the source of other people's dopamine? People's brain dopamine activity is highest when people are talking about themselves. So, get people to talk about themselves. Make them excited about what they are talking about. 'You are literally gifting dopamine during a podcast interview. You are trying to get them to have a mindgasm,' says Vanessa.

EXERCISE – First impressions

What is your one word that people would use to describe you when they first meet you? And what is the ideal first impression that you'd like to convey?

Why are they different? What is it about what you do or say or think or feel that is different?

Confidence

Among entrepreneurs and aspiring entrepreneurs that I coach, lack of confidence is the most common thing that they say prevents them from taking action. And of course if you didn't believe you would succeed, then why try? Here I'll attempt to help you understand where confidence comes from and how you can get more of it.

The three layers of confidence

I've developed a theory about confidence – think of it like layers of an onion, to which there are three levels, each based on different levels of our self-identity.

The outer layer is the charisma and body language portion, which we have covered so far in this chapter. This largely comes from our physical state, our bodies, how we carry ourselves, and how good we feel.

The second layer is a deeper level of identity that comes from our associations – who our friends are, the work we do, the organizations we are part of. Confidence at this level comes from feeling good about our place and role in the world. The third and deepest layer comes from an understanding of who we are. The international speaker, trainer and best-selling author, Ron Malhotra, told me that success comes from knowing ourselves. This layer can influence the other layers and underpins all confident behaviour. Once you establish this knowledge and confidence, it lasts. However, it is the level that is the most difficult to achieve since understanding of ourselves often only comes through great challenge and effort. As a man and adventurer, I'm still trying to prove to myself that age-old question: 'Do I have what it takes?'

How to acquire confidence

Your success in life is determined by the difficult conversations you are willing to have.
(Colleen Schell, Leadership expert, in our interview on The Art of Adventure)

Samuel Hatton of the Courageous Self Confidence podcast and I had a conversation about confidence. We agreed that confidence comes from experience, and at its core, is the conviction that you will be able to succeed in any circumstance. This includes your ability to learn new skills and have strong relationships with new people.

We want to move from domain specific to general confidence. If you are good at chess or guitar, that doesn't necessarily translate to mean you will be confident speaking to members of the opposite sex or going on TV. Just as with creative insights, we can move to the adjacent possible. Once you have confidence in one area, adjacent expertise feels less daunting as well.

A practice of adventurous thinking has the power to boost our confidence by familiarity with facing risk. By making it through a range of challenging scenarios, you build conviction in your own resourcefulness. Confidence helps give us a bias towards taking action, which is the only way to achieve positive career outcomes.

In the Lakota Indian tradition, as described in the book *Black Elk Speaks*, the warrior code mandates that at night around the camp-fire, the warriors are expected to tell tales of bravery and courage. Courage and bravery are the foundations that lead to confidence. You must have a practice of bravery that will lead you to try things that feel outside of your comfort zone that will slowly build your confidence. Confidence is a measure of experience and you cannot collect experience without sometimes pushing past the limits of your comfort zone. Luckily, this brings us again to the idea of the state of flow, or optimal experience.

Adventure always involves an element of risk, and therefore the adventurer becomes confident because he has gotten comfortable with discomfort. Carol Dweck outlines two ways of thinking in her book *Mindset: The Fixed Mindset and the Growth Mindset*. With the fixed mindset, we believe we are born with a certain amount of skill, smartness, beauty, etc. We must defend our level of all of these things at any cost, and if we make a mistake it means we are flawed. Mistakes in the growth mindset, however, are merely a symptom of learning. This allows us to take greater risks and know that we can grow in ability level through concerted effort. Only in realizing that our greatest achievements have come through grit and determination will we be comfortable putting in the effort.

If you think about confidence as knowledge – ie you know you will be able to accomplish what you set out to do, then that knowledge can only be gained by doing that very thing you set out to do. Therefore, confidence can only come through action.

EXERCISE – Unreasonable requests

Stephanie Burns, Founder of Chic CEO and *Forbes* columnist, taught me the idea of 'unreasonable requests'. How can you practise asking for things that might be outside of your comfort zone or you would expect to get a no to? Burns told me that it is often much easier to ask for big things for other people or causes that are important to you. For example, I have found that it is much easier to ask for money for charity than for myself. Making requests can lead to better outcomes. Ramit Sethi noted in his book *I Will Teach You To Be Rich*, that people are more likely to be compliant with your requests the more times you ask.

Here is how to practise making unreasonable requests. Start small – you can begin with asking to get your credit card fees waived or to have the seat you want in a restaurant. You can then ask for a free first-class upgrade or a free coffee. My friend's grandfather would always ask the cashier, 'How much is it with my discount?' Each day, challenge yourself to ask for something you normally wouldn't. In his TED talk, 'What I learned from 100 days of rejection,' Jia Jiang tells about his experience with asking for things. On his first day, he asked for a free hamburger refill, and later asked to make an announcement on an airplane. Jiang found that this practice allowed him to get past his fear, desensitize himself from the pain of rejection, and empowered him to practise courage as an entrepreneur.

EXERCISE – Micro adventures

One of the most common complaints I hear is that people want to have more fun in their lives. This exercise's outcomes can be twofold: we can have more fun while building our confidence using a series of #microadventures (term pioneered by National Geographic adventurer of the year, Alastair Humphreys). These are small daily challenges that you give yourself to take a risk.

Brainstorm: Ten ways that you can add adventure into the course of your normal daily life. Remember, adventure includes an element of risk, personal change and a good story.

International body language

While we value strong powerful body language in our leaders in the Western world, Asian cultures such as Japan have slightly different guidelines according to Kara Ronin. There is a strong deference for elders and superiors. So therefore, displaying strong confidence and powerful body language in the presence of someone higher up in our hierarchy could come across as impolite.

By studying what people perceive as confident and charismatic behaviours, you can begin to practise them and integrate them into your habits. Changing your posture or vocal tonality will feel abnormal at first, but eventually you will unconsciously portray high status signals. With these skills you can ace any interview, meet whoever you want to meet, and command the attention of a room.

We will take advantage of our newfound charisma skills when we start building relationships with people of power, influence and gravitas in the next chapter.

RESOURCES

Suggested further reading, books on charisma, confidence, and presence:

Fox Cabane, O (2013) *The Charisma Myth: How anyone can master the art and science of personal magnetism*

Hale Alter, C (2012) *Credibility Code: How to project confidence and competence when it matters most*

Hewlett, S A (2014) *Executive Presence: The missing link between merit and success*

Houpert, C (2014) *Charisma on Command: Inspire, impress, and energize everyone you meet*

Kay, K and Shipman, C (2014) *The Confidence Code: The science and art of self-assurance – what women should know*

Neffinger, J and Kohut, M (2014) *Compelling People: The hidden qualities that make us influential*

Pfeffer, J (2010) *Power: Why some people have it and some don't*

Port, M *Steal the Show: From speeches to job interviews to deal-closing pitches, how to guarantee a standing ovation for all the performances in your life*

Works cited

Cuddy, A. (2010) Power posing: brief nonverbal displays affect neuroendocrine levels and risk tolerance, *Psychological Science*, 1363–68

Gregoire, C (2016, 4 February) *Huffington Post*. Retrieved 16 February 2018, from www.huffingtonpost.com/entry/talking-with-hands-gestures_us_56afcfaae4b0b8d7c230414e

Harbinger, J (2015, February 2) The art of the interview and networking like a pro (D Loudermilk, interviewer)

Kohut, J N (2013) *Compelling People: The hidden qualities that make us influential*, Avery

Moyer, M W (2016, January 1) *Eye contact: How long is too long?* Retrieved 5 March 2018, from Scientific American: https://www.scientificamerican.com/article/eye-contact-how-long-is-too-long/

Robbins, T (2018, 16 February) *Tony Robbins*. Retrieved 16 February 2018, from www.tonyrobbins.com/health-vitality/the-power-of-cold-water/

Shevchuk, N (2008) Adapted cold shower as a potential treatment for depression, *Med Hypotheses*, 995–1001

Strack, F (1988) Inhibiting and facilitating conditions of the human smile: a nonobtrusive test of the facial feedback hypothesis, *Journal of Personality and Social Psychology*, 768–77

Trudeau, M (2010, September 20) *Human connections start with a friendly touch*. Retrieved 5 March 2018, from NPR: https://choice.npr.org/index.html?origin=http://www.npr.org/templates/story/story.php?storyId=128795325

08
Strategic relationships

I spent some time living in the town of Hoi An, Vietnam. It taught me some important lessons about relationships. Hoi An is a charming, world heritage designated, French colonial city in the middle of the country. Most days, I would walk around the corner from my apartment and have lunch with Hoia Linh, a local businessman who would make me a great meal of fried rice or Vietnamese pancakes for just a dollar. After lunch he would teach me to play Chinese Chess. After a couple weeks of learning with him (and secretly playing on my iPad at home) I started to get good enough to beat him. Hoia Linh decided it was time to take me to his favourite café. Picture a sprawling courtyard where a hundred men are playing board games, drinking coffee and watching soccer all day. Hoia Linh told me that these were all the most important people in town. When I asked how it could be that all the most successful people were not working during the middle of the day I learned a valuable lesson. Many of these business owners had hired inexpensive workers to man their shops and restaurants. Every once in a while, one would get a call that some tourists had entered the shop and the owner would race off on a motorbike to close the sale. It was whilst they were playing chess and hanging out, that the most important business deals would get made. If you needed a permit for a new building, furniture for your new restaurant or a fish supplier, this is the place you found what you needed. This coffee shop was where all the important decision makers were.

Outside of the small business world of Hoi An though, networking is just as important. According to the Carnegie Foundation and the

Stanford Research institute, technical skill and knowledge account for just 15 per cent of the reason you get, keep or advance in your job. The remaining 85 per cent of your job success rests on your ability to build great relationships with the people around you (Jensen, 2012).

You may have heard it said before that 'your network is your net worth'. The strength of your existing relationships determines how easily you will be able to find jobs, opportunities, funding, partners, clients or collaborators. That's why this chapter is going to explore how you can master building strong, strategic relationships in a powerful way that doesn't make you look sleazy or awkward.

The experts featured in this chapter

- We will hear from **Judy Robinette**, who has a fascinating personal story. She is from a small town in Idaho and now knows billionaires, investors, politicians and all kinds of people with wealth, gravitas and power. Judy says, 'Nothing happens without people. People are the ones that write the cheque, know about the opportunities, and know about the deals.'

- **Jordan Harbinger**, host of the Jordan Harbinger Show podcast has driven his business largely through networking.

- **Tyler Wagner** is the founder of Authors Unite, and author of the bestselling book *Conference Crushing*.

- **Jason Treu** is an author and coach, and known as the most connected person in Dallas, TX.

- **Garrison Cohen** will share his wisdom on how to host amazing events.

- **Travis Sheridan** shows us how to create an environment that supports innovation.

- **John Corcoran** is a former White House speech writer, and he will teach you exactly how to convert your relationships into business and opportunities.

- We will learn how **Jon Levy** founded the Influencer dinners and has had over 1,000 of the world's most influential people over for dinner, and how he was able to go from first-time author to a movie deal for his book *The 2 am Principle*.

I'll also share some of my own stories about how I have used relationships to talk my way into a PhD programme, find a house when moving my family to a new country, meet my heroes, and raise millions (of Indonesian Rupiah) for charity.

At the end of this chapter, you will have learnt how to:

- put together a strategic networking plan;
- build new relationships through generosity;
- find the superconnectors in your life to exponentially grow your network;
- be comfortable meeting new people;
- ask the right questions to get what you want;
- maximize attending live events;
- reach out to people online, even if they are busy and hard to reach; and
- use your relationships to drive business, bring in clients and get better at sales.

Strategic relationships

Most people have relationships with the people that they encounter on a regular basis: neighbours, work mates, the people in your weekend sports team. This is the no strategy approach. If you only rely on this proximity, you miss out on all kinds of potential relationships. A diverse and deep network is what to strive for. This means people who are different ages to you and who are in a diverse set of different career paths – anything from the arts, to law and even politics. You want to have relationships with people who have more experience than you do and people who are closer to the cutting edge than you.

I often tell clients to assemble a 'board of directors' for their life. Imagine if you had easy access to a venture capitalist, an industry journalist, an intellectual property lawyer, a local politician, a top web developer – you would be able to solve most of your problems with just a simple phone call!

Jim Rohn said: 'You are the average of the five people you spend the most time with.' It's been shown that happiness is contagious through at least 3 degrees of separation (So, 2009). The ideas and attitudes of people in your network will get into your own mind. You can carefully construct your worldview based on the people that you bring into your life. For example, I want to feel powerful, happy and creative, and that I can solve the hardest problems in my life. To that end, I make sure I have plenty of contact with people who already operate that way.

Judy Robinette says we should aim for a network that is wide, deep and robust. Wide means connections across geography, and across different industries whether it's media, TV, publishing, finance or any other. Robust means they will call you back, and deep means you have more than one connection in important relationship categories.

Maximizing your effort – meeting superconnectors

A superconnector is a person who, like many of the experts featured in this chapter, has a deep, wide and robust network. If you were to look at a visual map of the connections, these would be people who are like a hub of a wheel with spokes going out. Superconnectors can be journalists, politicians, charity members, restaurant owners, event organizers, venture capitalists, anyone whose position allows them to come in contact with lots of people. For clarity, the skills of the super-connector are a subset of being a Superconductor. Superconductors combine the other skills in this book such as creativity and acceler-ated learning with their relationships, in order to expand their impact.

But contact isn't the only requirement. Superconnectors focus on maintaining and growing strong relationships. They specialize in knowing how to help people, so they are always in a position of value. These can be some of the most effective and valuable people in your own network, because a superconnector can constantly supply you with opportunities and introductions.

EXERCISE – Find your superconnectors

Brainstorm and write down five superconnectors you already know, eg perhaps you know someone with a strong YouTube following, someone who does talks at high-profile conferences, or someone who writes for a major media company. Bonus: Write down ways you could add value to each of these people.

EXERCISE – Understand your network

Create a mindmap to visualize how all the people in your network are connected to each other. This will also help you identify superconnectors and other ways that you are making valuable connections.

Have a clear goal and get in the right room

Strategic relationship expert, Judy Robinett, has this great expression – to make the right connections, she said to me in our interview for the Art of Adventure, 'You need to get in the right room'. This means that you need to be part of organizations and events where your target audience goes. 'You can tell you're in the wrong room, if there isn't anyone smarter than you in that room, or anybody that can help you get to your goal. If they don't offer resources that can help you, you're in the wrong room.' Robinett suggests getting clear about what you need and finding out where the people that can help you hang out.

So if you are looking for investors, you need to be going to events where investors hang out. Think of it like going to the right marketplace – if you want to meet entrepreneurs that need new websites, where would these people spend time? Co-working spaces and entrepreneurship meet-ups would be a great place to start.

One unexpected example of getting in the right room for business is cycling groups. I grew up racing bicycles, and as an adult my cycling teammates and riding groups have presented me with countless opportunities. When I am back in my hometown of St Louis, I end up riding with my dad's cycling group. The others in the group are mostly aged between 40 and 60 and have highly successful careers, plenty of life experience, and a good deal of influence in the local community. Just being in contact with that group of 10 people has helped me get speaking gigs, publish this book, fund my charitable giving projects, and connect me with doctors to help my new-born baby. Similarly, when I came to Croatia, one of the first things I did was connect with the local cycling community here. I got invited on a big 140-km group ride, and on that ride I met some of the most influential local businesspeople, including some potential clients.

As much as possible we want to make our connections in person. If you have an online relationship and have the opportunity to meet in person, doing so can only deepen the relationship. Job offers, clients, collaborations are much more likely to happen if someone gets to know you in person. It is much easier to build trust that way. So where should you go to meet people? Bars? Networking events? Start by thinking about the kinds of activities that will attract the type of people you want to meet. Jason Treu says, 'The easiest way to start is go where influencers are, and people that are making this world move. This includes charities, nonprofits, museums, the arts, culture, that's where people who have money influence all go, and so go to those places and volunteer and get involved.'

What kind of opportunities are you looking for? Are you looking for a job, funding or a business partner? Different types of people are attached to these opportunities. If you are trying to find your dream job, for example, it makes sense to know employees in that organization who are already doing similar work, so you can understand how you might become a great candidate. Or by making friends with the hiring manager, you might learn about a position before it becomes available to the public. Another example: my network knows I have advertising space available on the Art of Adventure if the right sponsor were to come along, so when people have an idea of a company that might be a good fit, they simply give me the heads up or make an intro to the founder.

How many relationships should you aim for?

The anthropologist Robin Dunbar determined that 150 relationships was the amount that we as humans can maintain at any one time, based on the size and capacity of our brains. This is why you would see tribal groups split and separate as they grew past 150 people. Business units that are over 150 people become unwieldy and inefficient. Sure, you might be able to have thousands of Facebook friends, but we all have 24 hours in a day and can only realistically maintain a certain number of close connections. Robinett suggests having different levels in your top 150 connections: an inner circle of five people that you are talking to almost every day (best friends and family); a core of 45 people that you connect with weekly or monthly, that are your most valuable connections; and an extended network of the remaining 100 people that you connect with once a month or quarter that give your network its depth and breadth.

Your network gives you options

Jordan Harbinger is an amazing networker and host of the Jordan Harbinger Show. When I interviewed him he told me this story about when he started work as a new lawyer in New York City. Every new lawyer in the firm would be matched with a senior partner and go out for lunch together. However, Jordan's mentor was never in the office and it was hard finding a time to connect. When Jordan finally managed to get the partner to lunch, he asked him a burning question: how is it that he never seemed to be in the office, but still made more money than all the other partners?

The partner explained that instead of spending all his time in the office he was out making connections: playing golf, attending charity events, going for lunches. This was how he brought in the business that allowed everyone else to get paid. The partner knew that if the law firm folded, he could simply walk right down the street and into a new job the very next day because of his relationship skills.

John Corcoran got his speech-writing job in the White House by establishing a network with other speechwriters. John told me about his strategy in our interview: 'For the speech writers, I'd find other speeches that I would send to them, or poems, articles, or little bits of inspiration that I thought that they could use in their work. I'd send them things from time to time to keep top of mind, and eventually an opportunity for a writing job came along and one of the speech writers gave me the heads up.' Corcoran established his network and generosity before he needed it so that he could take advantage when the right opportunity arose.

Connecting with people online

Say I want to form a relationship with someone I only know online. I start by taking a look at their website, Instagram, Twitter and recent blog posts to understand what their world is like and what is on their mind? Think of it like researching them like you would for an interview. Why do you want to meet with this person? Do you want them to mentor you, collaborate with you, introduce you to someone or become a customer?

When I interviewed Jason Treu, he gave me some valuable practical tips on how to meet people online. 'Make a list of about 20 or 30 people that you want to go after, and that are strategic for you to meet for whatever reason. Then what I would do is for about two weeks, interact with them on their social media and blog and make thoughtful comments on there.'

It is really easy to reach out to someone on Twitter. Start engaging with their tweets. Or their blog posts, or their Instagram, or their podcast. What this means is leaving meaningful comments; supporting them with your presence. I've made some amazing connections through leaving thoughtful comments that contribute to a valuable discussion and even simply by liking posts. Make genuine comments about things that you like and agree with and you'll avoid appearing creepy or artificial.

It's often easier to make connections if you have something to offer the other person. Sometimes I find guests for my show by reaching out on Twitter and saying – 'Hey! I'd love to have you as a guest on the podcast. Are you interested?' This means they just have to say Yes or No. We can sort out the details in email.

You want to make it as easy as possible for this new person to connect back with you. If they say yes to your opportunity, that means they are interested and are pre-committing to helping you or even to being your friend. Don't send them your life story in an email and don't ask them for something big or time-consuming up front. Getting a simple reply sets up further conversations that are up to you to lead into the next steps of the relationship.

Jason Treu also recommends sending emails that don't ask questions that put the person you're trying to connect with under pressure to respond: I have talked to a lot of influencers and they get overwhelmed with emails they can't respond to. Then it makes them feel guilty and then they never respond, and so now you're a person who they feel guilty about and that creates a distance.' Instead, he advises you to comment on the positive impact their work has had on you and what results you've been able to achieve by following them.

In my interview with Caroline Weiler, she told me she met her business partner Sylvie on Instagram. They run the successful Travel Storytelling Festival. They just liked what each other were up to and started commenting and sharing ideas and pretty soon they had a business partnership.

EXERCISE – Building a team that complements your skills

Take the Wealth Dynamics personality test or other career assessment. Find out what type of person you are and find the other types of people who would make ideal team members. Then refer to your networking mind map and find those people in your network and invite them to your team or project.

Relationship building example: moving to a new country

When my family moved to Zadar, Croatia in 2017, we knew that we would need to build relationships quickly so we could feel at home in our new city. On arrival we learned that it was going to be hard to find a house to rent for three months because everyone was saving space to rent their rooms and houses during high season when prices quadruple.

In the first 24 hours we met up with Martina and she became our first friend. I had connected with her on Instagram and invited her to share her project – The Zadar outdoor festival on the Art of Adventure podcast. Martina then introduced us to her colleague Iva, who was managing a house that she needed to fill. It was a huge 250-year-old stone house in a quiet neighbourhood close to the beach and was everything we wanted in a house. We moved in within a day.

To connect with more of the English-speaking community, I joined a Zadar expat Facebook group and recorded a 60-second live video introducing our family and describing who we were looking to meet. Through that short video we met an American whose boyfriend is the star centre of the professional basketball team and they offered to take us to a playoff game. We also met the owner of a hostel who lived in our neighbourhood who told us how to get internet on our phones, which café had the best coffee and offered us the use of their car.

I was also looking to grow my business so I reached out to the manager of the local co-working space in Zadar and offered to speak there. I met Slavica and she told me how to pitch myself to the four government agencies who shared ownership of the co-working space and in just a couple of days I had multiple offers to speak.

By building relationships I was able to solve most of our practical needs upon moving to a new country and find new opportunities for my business.

How to take advantage of Facebook groups

I love to take advantage of Facebook groups. Most of them are free and are focused around a specific interest. Groups I have been a part of include groups for coaches, authors, entrepreneurs, cyclists, digital nomads and expats.

I usually start with a video introduction of myself, telling people what I am up to and why I am in the group. I talk about what types of people I am looking to connect with, my interests, and share some fun little facts about me. Then I offer to help the group. I'll offer to review someone's product on Amazon or subscribe to their podcast, or give advice about business or travel. This way I put myself out there first (and take advantage of Facebook's algorithm preference for video) and see who resonates with me. Often some of the first people I encounter in this way become long-term friends and some become business collaborators or future podcast guests.

These groups are great places to ask specific advice and get support (emotionally or strategically). I usually check the group every other day or so and if there are questions that I can answer quickly, I will type a response; additionally I'll offer to get on the phone with someone to give them more detailed advice. Ideally you find at least a group of people who are at your same career level, so you can keep each other accountable for your progress, learn from each other, and brainstorm together. If you ask for help in the group and you get good advice, follow up with a post of how you used that advice and what the outcome was, so other people with similar questions can see how it went for you. We learn from each other, so some of the best posts are about problems you have solved or lessons you have learned.

EXERCISE – Create a video introduction

If you aren't in any Facebook groups, join one that is in your career area. Next, draft a 90-second script to introduce yourself to the group. Use your elevator pitch that you constructed from the storytelling chapter as a starting point. Tell people why you joined the group, who you help, who you are looking to meet, and something interesting about yourself that will allow people to connect with you.

How I use podcasting as a relationship-building tool

It's always good to have a win-win framework to meet people that you want to meet. In the four years that I have been running the Art of Adventure podcast, it has become one of the best ways for me to connect with people that I want to include in my network of relationships.

I benefit from the journalistic privilege of being able to reach out to someone and ask them questions. Because the podcast reaches thousands of listeners, there is an immediate and obvious value that I am providing. I start with a list of all the people that I would love to learn from as a guest on the podcast and people that would be great for my audience of entrepreneurs, travellers, digital nomads and adventurers.

The best way to meet someone is by a personal introduction. I often ask friends and acquaintances if they know a specific person or type of person. For example, if I wanted to know more about relationship building for this chapter, I would put a message out to my network and ask who the best networker they know is. If I don't have a contact that knows them, I will get in touch by several means, often simultaneously: email, Twitter, Instagram, their website's contact form, the contact form on their webpage, LinkedIn, Quora.

After an hour conversation on the show, we have built rapport and trust and it opens the door for a continued relationship. I usually have a good sense of how I might be able to help them and I will take the last five minutes of our call to offer selected introductions, resources or organizations I think they might find interesting.

Preparing for conferences or events

One of the best ways to meet people in person is at conferences and live events. No matter what industry interest group you are in, there are events that cater to your tribe.

Tyler Wagner breaks down his approach to getting the most from attending live events into the before, during and after phases. These are Tyler and Jason's best practices, with my notes:

Before the event

- **Know yourself** – define the skills, talents, and knowledge you bring to the table in relation to the types of people that you will be meeting at the event. This will make it easier to notice opportunities to provide value to other people at the event.

- **Do your homework** – who would you like to meet at the event? Check out their website, Twitter and Instagram so you get to know their interests. Start with the organizers of the event and the influential speakers that you want to connect with. Often there is a Facebook group for the event where you can engage with people beforehand. If I am speaking at an event, I will usually reach out and connect with all the other speakers prior to the event.

- **Define your goals** and come up with a concrete plan for the event. A good goal can be as simple as building one solid new relationship.

- **Add surprising value before you go.** One of the best ideas I have heard of is to summarize in more detail the research you have done about the speakers. You can send this out to all attendees or post in the Facebook group. I saw someone do this after the Podcast Movement conference – they compiled key takeaways from each ✓ talk they attended to help people who had missed some of the talks.

- **Set meetings ahead of time**. You can stand out from the crowd because most people don't set meetings ahead of time. It also saves you from having to go hunt someone down.

During the event

1 Take advantage of the skills you learned in Chapter 7 to maximize your in-person interactions.

2 Make a list to remind yourself of the things you should avoid doing at the conference. Getting too drunk or forgetting to keep track of who you have talked to, for example.

3 Ask for introductions. 'Who do you think I should meet?' This works best with superconnectors such as the event host or speakers.

4 Get out of your comfort zone and participate as much as possible.

5 Be a mini organizer within the event. For instance, podcaster Jaime Masters hosted a UFC fight night viewing during the Podcast Movement conference.

6 Help make people comfortable. Go out of your way to include people.

7 Be authentic in your conversations. Ask open-ended questions: What's on your agenda for the week? What have you been up to this summer? Do you have any cool trips planned? What projects are you working on right now that you are really passionate about? Who is your hero? (The secret bonus here is that you might be able to introduce them to their hero.)

8 Take notes about who you meet and what you learn.

9 Volunteer. If you work the check-in desk, you can also meet people as they're walking in and set up later conversations. You will also get familiar with the event before it starts to help you feel more comfortable.

After the event

1 Review your notes! This will help with introductions and personalized follow-ups.

2 Write handwritten letters to people.

3 Follow up with people you have met at the conference. For example, by sending an email, calling them, sending them a video of you or mailing them a personalized gift (I like to send books).

4 Maintain your network. Use a CRM, spreadsheet, or any other tools and reminders to help you maintain those connections you have established.

What to do if you are nervous about meeting people

Are you worried that people won't like you? Let me dispel that idea right now. I'm a new father – my son is a year old, and I love him so much, just for being who he is. He can't even have a conversation yet – he just smiles and plays. He doesn't have to do anything special to be loved, and neither do you. But you have several advantages over babies – you can engage in thoughtful conversations. You can help people.

And don't worry if you are an introvert – some of the best network-ers are introverts. I have a lot of introvert tendencies myself – I love people, but being around too many for too long drains me. I have to be careful to limit my exposure and recover in between so that I can be cheerful and engaging when I'm present. At conferences, you can often find me hiding out in my room in the middle of the afternoon.

Judy Robinette told me that once she learned that people really did like her, it motivated her to engage with people wherever she goes. 'If you have been to Montana, when you enter the state it says, "Howdy stranger!" I love that as a way to think about meeting people.' Robinette told me how to practise engaging with new people. 'Start with the people you encounter during the course of your day. Maybe it is someone captive in a bank line next to you, or on a plane, and if you just start saying hello, or smiling at people, you'll notice people warm up instantly, and pretty soon you're engaging in conversations, and then you get braver, and you find out that people like you.'

Curating experiences and events

We have already established that going to live events and meeting people in person are some of the fastest ways to build rapport and trust in new relationships. But what about hosting your own events? Being the organizer or host of an event means that you become the hub, the superconnector, for that group of people.

In my interview with Garrison Cohen, we talked about the community he has created globally by hosting regular events and parties. When I met Garrison in Bali, he was organizing an American Thanksgiving dinner complete with the traditional roast turkey, cranberry sauce and stuffing. The dinner ended up being about 50 people, and Garrison was able to get a local restaurant to supply all the meals and he gave a big speech about the history of thanksgiving for all the non-Americans. The whole event lasted several hours with lots of games and community building.

Here are some of the events Garrison is known for:

- *Awesomeness Party*. Everyone has to bring their most awesome friend.

- *Wedding Characters Party* – where everyone comes as stereotypical characters you might find at a wedding.
- *Parents Party*. Everyone invites their parents.
- *Stylish Friends Clothing Swap*. Garrison has a lot of successful stylish male friends in San Francisco and has a gathering where everyone gets to swap clothes. If there is an item you like, you can claim it, but someone else can challenge you if they like it as well, and then you have a fashion show and the group decides who it looks better on.
- *Signature Dish Cooking Party*.
- *Progressive Party*. 200 friends move from house to house around the neighbourhood, each house hosting a different type of food.
- *Celebrity Judge Cookoff*.

Some of the theme parties that I have had success with are:

- rock paper scissors tournament;
- cocktail contest;
- chalk art; and
- charity dance party.

Jon Levy built his extensive network by hosting dinner parties. Levy is known as the creator of the Influencers Dinner. At this point he has had over 1,000 people at his dinner events and salons. He invites high level and interesting people he knows but who don't know each other. They are only allowed to know each other's first name and they can't talk about what they do until after they all prepare dinner together. Then at dinner they have to guess what each person does.

The idea is that because the guests are participating in a shared activity, they are able to bond and build relationships before they find out what each person does for a living. How does he get these busy and important people to come to his events? Most people he invites say yes. A little proof of concept goes a long way. He was featured in the *New York Times* and points to that as verification that it is a worthwhile use of their time.

You can take the same idea and apply it to your own connections – inviting friends and contacts from across disparate networks to attend an event you organize, however low key. If you can be a curator of people and host events, then you become the hub of many other people's networks.

Charity and community events can also be excellent ways of bringing people together and enhancing your own network in a sustainable and positive way. You win twice by being thoughtful and inviting someone to an event they will love, and you win again when they meet the other people you have invited. Combining this with volunteering with an organization you admire can put you in contact with a ton of the right people.

Travis Sheridan, the global director of Venture Café, has built his business on events that connect people. Venture Café is a weekly event that happens every Thursday, 49 weeks a year in cities around the globe. Hundreds of people attend the free workshops, get free beer, and share ideas. The motto of Venture Café is 'Connecting Innovators to Make Things Happen'. Venture Café is now the place where people come to make the right connections. A regular event can build your personal reputation.

Starting a new relationship

Here is an example flow for cultivating a relationship.

1 Finding the person you want to meet and research them online.

2 Making your initial connect electronically or when you are together in the same location.

3 Being generous and completing a five-minute favour.

4 Making introductions and promoting their work.

5 Hosting them to speak if they are visiting your city.

6 Having deep conversations with them, and being a good listener.

7 Exchanging book recommendations.

Tools to enhance your relationship building

The three golden questions

Judy Robinette introduced me to the idea of the three golden questions as a way of enhancing your relationships.

1 She explained: 'First, you share a little bit about your story. My goals for this year are A, B and C. Then you ask question number one: What other ideas do you have for me?' In her experience this allows people to get creative and it's really interesting to see what people will come up with.

2 The second question she says you should ask is: 'Who else do you know I should talk to?' According to Judy, on average people know 632 other people and it's likely that they will know someone who can help you with your goals.

3 Robinette's third golden question is 'How can I help you?' You can go one step further and come up with an idea for how to help them and ask: 'Would it be helpful if I did X for you?' Giving value to other people helps to build your relationship with them and can lead to great opportunities.

The five-minute favour

This is the idea that Adam Grant proposed in his book *Give and Take*. A five-minute favour is anything you can do that will be immediately beneficial to the other party and won't take much of your time. Jason Treu says, 'Generosity is the fastest way to build trust with someone.'

Offering to do a favour could be connecting them with someone that could help them, forwarding them an opportunity you've seen that you think matches their goals or sending them some information you have that could help them with the project they're working on.

Jason suggests offering a favour by saying: 'Hey, I'll send you some stuff, I got some ideas', or, 'I'll think about it, and I'll follow back up with you.' When you give first, then people like you immediately, and that puts you in a place of power and influence. It works every single time.

I was speaking in Belgium at the Travel Storytelling Festival and one local attendee came to my talk and afterwards reached out and offered to design a couple of things for my website. A couple of buttons that he noticed could be improved. He customized them to match my site, it looks great and now we have a relationship. I'd answer his email right away if he ever asked me for something.

Cultivate empathy

When I ask guests at the end of the Art of Adventure, what they would most like to change or add to the world, empathy is the most common response. We are all seeking to be understood, so if you can understand others, co-workers, partners and employees, you will give yourself a superpower in that they will be open to hearing you.

An epic five-minute favour

When I interviewed John Corcoran, he highlighted the importance of being able to have a good conversation with high-level people. With a little thought and knowledge about what that person likes or finds interesting, you can customize your interaction to delight them. John did precisely this and ended up having a valuable conversation with US president Bill Clinton at a ceremony at the White House.

Corcoran told me, 'We found out beforehand that President Clinton was building up his DVD collection because he'd just gotten a DVD player. This was back in 2000, and he really liked old westerns. So, we went and we bought a couple of old westerns... put a bow on top of them and waited until we got up to the front of this huge line of people that wanted to get pictures with him. When we got up to the front, we gave him the DVDs and ended up having a five- or six-minute conversation with him about old Western movies. All the VIPs behind us were thinking, "wait a second, everyone else is rushing through but these guys? Who are these guys?"' This is an amazing story because it means that with a little research and thoughtful planning, you can connect with the most important people in the world.

EXERCISE – Five-minute favours

Brainstorm at least 10 different ways that you can provide a five-minute favour to new and existing connections. Who can you introduce them to? What information might be valuable to them? What ideas could help their business? How has their work positively impacted you? Can you recommend a book or restaurant to them? Can you give them a public shout-out?

Bonus: Email introduction template you can use for five-minute favours:

Hi (Person 1) and (Person 2),

I'd like to introduce you! Optional background on how you met each person/your personal connection.

(Person 1), (Person 2) Does X Y Z and I think you would like to meet them because of (reasons)?

(Person 2), (Person 1) Does X Y Z and I think you would like to meet them because of (reasons)?

(Person 2) (whoever has more to gain from the connection), I'll leave it to you to follow up!

Stay Adventurous!

(Your Name)

The art of asking – let people help you

Having a few easy things that people can help you with is great; it's a service to them. Have a ready quiver of things you can ask for. Have a mission or goal that people can get behind and support.

Ben Franklin strategically asked for favours to help build his team of supporters. He would ask people to borrow a book from their personal collection. Because of the principle of consistency, people that do a small favour for you are more likely to do a bigger favour for you in the future. Unconsciously they think, 'I must like this person if I am doing favours for them, and I help people that I like.' This principle was described by Robert Cialdini in his book *Influence*, and builds upon small initial commitments.

For example, if people ask me how they can help me, the easiest thing for them to do is to subscribe to the Art of Adventure podcast and leave a rating and review. It helps the show move up in the rankings and get out to more people. It takes just a minute or two. What is something that people can help you with in a minute or two? Have a couple of five-minute favours you can give people to do for you.

There is an amazing book by Amanda Palmer called the *Art of Asking*, which I read about the time I first learned I was going to be a father. The day I found out I was going to be a dad, I was feeling really sick, feeling like I couldn't handle the challenge. I was getting the cold sweats and feeling like I wanted to vomit but couldn't. I realized I was going to need to ask for help and lots of it. Advice from men who were already dads, support from my friends and family, support from my male friends, I had to learn to ask for clients more quickly because I needed to support my family.

Jason Treu told me that he has struggled with asking people for help as well: 'That's one of my greatest weaknesses is doing the asking, and I realize this, and I'm trying to work on that. Giving someone the opportunity to help you is actually a great service. People want to help (they have told me), they often just don't know how, or don't want to intrude on your life. So you have to be proactive in how you communicate and just ask.'

To get comfortable with asking, refer to the exercise in Chapter 7.

How to turn relationships into business opportunities

Building meaningful relationships is valuable in itself. However, if you are looking for opportunities you need to take advantage of the hard work you've done in making connections. Let's look at how you can use your relationships to help you reach your goals.

I asked John Corcoran about this, because he is a master networker and it helps power his business pursuits. He told me, 'One of the things that I recommend people do is to look back at your referrals, if you depend on the referrals for your living, which a lot of people do. If you actually track it you'll probably find this came from attending some specific conference, or from my friendship with so and so, or from this group that I belong to that I communicate with on Facebook.'

He has done this in his own business and noticed that a real estate agent that had forwarded several clients to him in the past wasn't sending him new referrals. He realized he hadn't been in contact with her for nine months so he invited her to have coffee and a week later she referred more business leads to him. Once you see how you're getting your business opportunities then you know which relationships you should be prioritizing.

EXERCISE – Who makes you money?

Go to the mind map of your relationships and highlight in green all the people who have referred business to you, or have helped you find a job, or have made you money in some way. These are the relationships you want to pay special attention to. When was the last time you connected with them? If it has been longer than a month, schedule a time to email, call, or do a five-minute favour for them. Let them know how much you appreciate their positive impact on your career or business.

EXERCISE – Building a team that complements your skills

Take the Wealth Dynamics personality test or other career assessment. Find out what type of person you are and find the other types of people who would make ideal team members. Then refer to your networking mind map and find those people in your network and invite them to your team or project.

How I networked my way into graduate school

Back in 2011, I wanted to diversify my career and go to graduate school to study extremophiles. I spent an hour each morning for several months looking up all the cool things that scientists at major universities were doing. Then, I would email or call them to ask about their work.

At first, I wasn't getting much of a response, so I started systematically testing different emails to see what would get the best response rates. One of the keys to getting good responses back was to specifically state the one part of their work that I was most interested in and ask them about it. Sometimes I would share a recent (one week old) journal article that they might be interested in. Eventually, after a few email exchanges, I was able to set up a couple of phone interviews.

I decided that Montana State had the best collection of scientists who thought like me and were doing the work I wanted to do. I decided to fly up and introduce myself in person. I emailed all the professors I had already been in contact with and was able to set up nine meetings on a three-day trip. I took a lot of notes, and had a lot of questions ready, tailored to each scientist I talked to. My last meeting was with the department chair. I laid out my main points of why I wanted to go to MSU, how well I would fit in and what I would achieve, and made sure to mention all the professors I had talked to. The next morning my acceptance letter was in my inbox!

Here are the key elements from my example that you can use:

1 Sometimes it makes sense to fly somewhere to make in-person connections.

2 Let other people that like you speak on your behalf.

3 Do your homework and tell people how you will be useful to them.

4 Test different ways to get the attention of the people you want to meet.

5 Choose your surroundings carefully for the outcome you are hoping for.

6 Ask for what you want and have a plan to back it up.

Conclusion

By now you are probably more motivated than ever to go out and meet amazing people who can help your business and life goals. You have learned about how to think of strategic relationships, how to meet people online and in person, how to take advantage of events as a host or a participant, you have heard some stories about how people use their relationship connections to get what they want in life. In the next chapter, you will learn about how to be more charismatic and confident when you are meeting people.

Works cited

Jensen, K (2012, April 12) *Forbes*. Retrieved 9 April 2018, from Intelligence Is Overrated: What You Really Need To Succeed: www.forbes.com/sites/keldjensen/2012/04/12/intelligence-is-overrated-what-you-really-need-to-succeed/#56498f4cb6d2

So, T (2009, 18 November) *The Three Degrees of Influence and Happiness*. Retrieved 6 March 2018, from *Positive Psychology News*: http://positivepsychologynews.com/news/timothy-so/200911185246

09
Think big

If you could change or add anything to the world, what would you wish for the world to have?

FINAL QUESTION TO GUESTS ON THE ART OF ADVENTURE PODCAST

No great world-changing innovation has ever been created by someone that did not have a dream or wanted to preserve the status quo. Before anything can become reality, we must dream it. The basic idea behind the popular book *Think and Grow Rich* (Hill, 1937) or the idea of manifestation from the movie *The Secret* is that before you can make big things happen, you need to envision them.

Tim Ferriss often points out that the bigger you think, the more your competition drops away. This is because people take themselves out of the game because they assume taking on a big challenge will be harder than taking on a small one. Let's assume that you are not thinking big enough. And that is the case because of your own limited worldview. Don't worry – we are all limited in some ways by our life experience. The point is you can use creative thinking or even get outside input on how to think bigger.

Dreaming big does one magic thing: it is like pouring gasoline on a fire. Big dreams are rocket fuel. They propel you forwards with tremendous excitement. Think about this – the different levels of excitement from posting a blog post with your dreams vs. standing on the steps of the Washington Monument in Washington DC and giving a speech to hundreds of thousands of people.

A desire to make an impact is now a major driver of people's career choices, and organizations everywhere are helping their employees think bigger about their impact. Aaron Hurst, founder of Imperative, told me in our interview for the Art of Adventure that companies that are purpose-driven show 400 per cent higher performance, and individual employees show 125 per cent higher productivity when they are aligned with purpose. For example, IDEO created IDEO.org to solve poverty-related challenges by offering their talented designers to communities who need them the most and Whole Foods created Community Giving Days where 5 per cent of that day's net sales are given to local non-profits (Hewitt, 2013).

In this chapter, we will cover some ways that big dreams and big thinking can help your career. Firstly, thinking big and acting on your goals will differentiate you from those who are not so bold. You are going to learn how to start planning and taking action on your big goals, even before you see the whole picture on how to make them happen. You will learn how to build a team to support you and how to build conviction in your projects so you can support yourself. You will learn how to assess the skills you need to acquire to make your dreams happen, and how to get access to bigger dreams than you could have imagined. We will explore the power of finding a specific person to fight for, so that you make your dreams real and meaning-ful. You will learn how to plan for the worst, so that you can prepare for the best. You will learn the power of bringing a big dream to other people and sharing your vision. And you will learn to own your big dreams as part of your personality.

Crazy is a compliment

Linda Rottenberg is the author of *Crazy Is a Compliment* and the founder of Endeavor, which supports dreamers and doers around the world through mentorship. Linda told me, 'The greatest barrier to getting going is psychological.' Because she also had risk averse people in her life, she recognized that often, people need permission to start dreaming big.

These days, dreaming big is not just for political leaders or entre-preneurs. Linda told me on the podcast, 'If you are not being called crazy, then you are not thinking big enough.' Henry Ford was known as 'Crazy Henry' for always tinkering with cars in his back yard, and Jack Ma was called 'Crazy Jack', 15 years before he took Alibaba.com public. When she was first talking about the idea to start Endeavor, her parents did everything they could to talk her out of it. She had to ask herself, 'Am I going to do what my parents expect me to do, or am I going to try this idea that I don't know is going to work? I had to choose hope instead of fear.' If you are working for a corporation, don't ask permission right away to follow your ideas. Operate in stealth mode for a while until you have a solid proof of concept. You want to make it easy for your superiors to get behind a project and look good.

Leverage

If you are going to think big, you will want to access the most powerful tools and ideas at your disposal. Author Erica Dhawan told me that connectional intelligence is about leveraging knowledge and networks in new ways. For example, how might you get more from the communities you are already part of? With increased connectivity, we have access to new ways of thinking about problems. Dhawan put it to me this way, 'Instead of thinking outside the box, create a bigger box and bring people in to think with you.'

How can you leverage what you already know and care about for bigger uses? How can you leverage your existing relationships? How can you leverage your existing communities? Dhawan advises us to first dream big, then add connection (resources, disciplines, ideas), get curious, use courage, and then adjust your dream even bigger. I see it as a virtuous cycle – maximizing your leverage helps you think bigger, and thinking bigger forces you to use all the leverage at your disposal to solve your problem.

You don't have to see all the steps

It's ok to not know how your big dreams will happen. First, if your dream is similar enough to what someone else has achieved, then that is basically proof that it is possible. If no one has ever done what you are dreaming of, then look to all the other times in history where something was created out of nothing.

When you climb a mountain, you can generally see the summit, and you can see the trail as it starts in front of you. But you can't see the trail up ahead around the bend or when it disappears into the forest.

Likewise, you might not be able to know all the steps it will take you to achieve your big dreams. Only after taking many steps, will the next part of your journey become illuminated. And just like climbing a mountain, there are many different possible routes you can take to achieve a big dream. So it's not the 'How' that is important, it is the 'What', and the 'Why' that will drive your success. Having clarity on these two parts will help spur you into taking action.

Businesswoman and author Linda Rottenberg told me about the power of 'Thinking big but executing small'. The challenge of successful dreamers is to break down big challenges into a series of small wins. In his historic podcast with Marc Maron, President Obama made the analogy of changing US political policy to attempting to steer a giant boat like an aircraft carrier – you make a one degree change now so that in 15 years you see a big difference. Think of taking action on your dreams like the power of compound interest. If you make a 1 per cent improvement or progress each day, by the end of the year you are at more than 400 per cent.

EXERCISE – Pick your big hairy audacious goal

Think of a goal that is so big that you can't see how it will be possible. The right goal creates a feeling that is somewhere between fear and excitement. It's important that you don't need this goal to happen – it won't affect your health or happiness. A big goal is just a goal until you start thinking about it in concrete terms.

What are the five major moves to achieving this goal? What are the costs associated to making this goal happen. What do you expect to have to give? Who do you have to BE to achieve this goal? What type of structure do you need in your life to support you with this goal. (A coach? An accountability buddy? Financial stakes? Join a mastermind?)

Build conviction

When you are absolutely convinced your big goal is the right thing to do and you believe without a doubt that it will happen, the only thing left to do is to take action. But when you are not 100 per cent convinced that you are heading in the right direction, or whether you will succeed, you will intentionally put the breaks on until you feel ready. You will sabotage your own work because you aren't convinced you can do it, so you want to prove to yourself that you are right. As you get good results from taking action, you continue to reinforce your conviction.

EXERCISE – 100 reasons why you will succeed

To prove to yourself that you will succeed, come up with a list of 100 reasons why you will and deserve to succeed. Like a lawyer preparing his case or a mathematician preparing a proof, you need to use only true statements. I have my clients do this exercise at times when they raise their prices or are offering a new product or service. Customers can tell your level of conviction in your voice when you offer your solution to them. When you can get to the point where you think people are crazy not to buy from you/hire you/partner with you, etc. You will have a much easier time getting them on board.

So let's say your goal is to start a podcast. Some points of factual evidence that will prove to you that it is possible: 'Other people have launched podcasts already; podcasts are cheap to start and I have enough money to start one; I know someone with a podcast who I can ask for advice; I am good at asking questions; I can be more useful if I amplify my message, etc...' Once you get to 100 reasons, I expect your confidence in your ability to achieve your big goal to be rock solid.

You need a team

The biggest goals in the world simply cannot be accomplished by a single person. For example, the Bill and Melinda Gates foundation has more than 1,300 employees to help them manage their tens of billions of dollars in charitable giving.

Business advisor and author Monty Hooke similarly told me, 'There is a ceiling to what you can create on your own'. Monty created EZY VA, an organization that helps Entrepreneurs by pairing them with virtual assistants.

As the founder of CD Baby, Derek Sivers knew that there was too much for him to do alone. He started creating procedures for every function that he did, so that any one of his employees could pick up the manual of operating procedures and get the same results. Essentially, Sivers prepared to replace himself.

Whether you go by the Myers–Briggs test or some other personality assessment, there are many different types of people. When you are building teams, find people who are nearly opposite you in terms of personality type, because they will complement your style. A team get stronger by having both visionaries and detail-oriented people, deal makers and fine tuners (Hamilton, nd).

If you determine you need a team, the next step is to move into action. Who have you told that is on board with your big goal? Do you need to hire people to support this vision? Do you need to find a business partner? Maybe you need an angel investor with money and the right experience to help you.

EXERCISE – Who do you need?

Take the Wealth Dynamics personality test. Find out what type of person you are and find the other types of people who would make ideal team members. Then refer to your networking mind map from Chapter 8 and find those people in your network and invite them to have a conversation about your project with an eye towards bringing them onto your team.

Find out where your vision is limited

There are known knowns. There are things we know that we know. There are known unknowns. That is to say, there are things that we now know we don't know. But there are also unknown unknowns. There are things we do not know we don't know.

(Former US Secretary of Defense Donald Rumsfeld in Logan, 2009)

One of my clients was planning a trip to Thailand from the US for her graduate degree. She is a speaker and I suggested she give a couple of talks while in Bangkok. She said, 'You mean I can be an international speaker?' Nobody ever told her that she could do that, and it never crossed her mind to consider it. Nobody thought breaking the four-minute mile was possible until Roger Bannister broke it, and now it gets broken every week. Nobody thought that becoming a billionaire was possible until someone did it and now Elon Musk is on track to become the first trillionaire.

Maybe your big vision is limited by your life experience, or maybe your big vision is limited by how much you let yourself be free with your thoughts. Are you giving yourself permission to go big? Or are you holding back in case your dreams don't come true? If you are already achieving as much as you can at your current skill level, your big vision might exceed your capabilities at this point. Don't let your current state of skill, life experience, or personality limit your vision. Experience and skills are things you can go and acquire as needed in service of your objective. Personality is something that always continues to evolve.

Planning big

Thinking and dreaming big must be matched with big plans. If you don't have clear objectives and steps with deadlines on your calendar, you are still just dreaming. The system and structure in your life right now are perfect to get you where you are. To go somewhere new and bigger, you will need systems and structure that give you different outputs.

Perfectionism is the worst enemy of the dreamer because it prevents us from taking action. It keeps us in dreaming mode rather than moving into doing mode. At some point once you have dreamed your big vision, you need to come up with a plan of action, the steps that you will take, and then you need to set aside the time and actually take those steps.

We overestimate what we can accomplish in a day and underestimate what we can get done in a year. By applying the adventure mindset to our dreams, we create a bias towards action. When I was training racing cyclists, one of the first things I taught them was that success as a racer wasn't about one good workout a week where they would go out and absolutely exhaust themselves, it was about progression and a concerted effort towards their big goal. With things like changing our physiology, it actually takes time to build the new tissues we need. To achieve big dreams, it's about the aggregate of our efforts. It's better to have a small win every day for a month than one big day. Each small win increases our skill, confidence, experience, and if you set up good systems for yourself, makes the next challenge a little bit easier.

Planning your skills

By now you know that you can achieve so much more by stacking and perfecting the right skills to achieve your goals. When you start planning how you will achieve your big dreams, think about what skills you will need to develop in order to make them possible. Sometimes a dream is so big that it might take multiple levels of dreaming to make it happen. I have a big dream of hosting a global conference that brings together thought leaders to solve global problems and eventually becomes its own education curriculum. One of the key skills will be my ability to manage a complex live event. In order to work up to that, I am running a series of smaller events such as workshops and AdventureQuest trips.

Understand worst-case scenarios

Dreaming big isn't about ignoring reality. There is a chance you could fail. Many of us get hung up on the downside potential rather than the upside potential because we don't fully understand what the worst-case scenario really is. So let's take a close look at what the true worst-case scenario is. Tim Ferriss calls this practice 'fear setting' and says that it is one of the most important drivers of his success.

Let's take a look at my big dream for the Global Goal genius Gathering (or G4, which hasn't happened yet). If I spent an entire year focusing on putting together the first event, building the organizing team, finding the funding, getting speakers, planning the schedule, and it completely failed, what are the real risks? I might give up hundreds of thousands of dollars in earnings from other components of my business. I might spend some of my relationship capital asking people to support the project. I might get really burnt out from working hard. But on a scale of 1–10, the worst that would probably happen would be a 3 or 4. And the upside potential of having this conference take off (even if it is a partial execution of the complete vision the first time) is a 9 or 10 – we really could change the world.

Understanding the worst-case scenario helps us be prepared for it, even while we know that it is unlikely to happen. When you understand the worst-case scenario – that your venture might not work, will you be able to go back to the position you were in? Will you be able to get a similar position going and restart your baseline? For most people this is a yes.

Now that we have determined the worst-case scenario, can we put any limits in place that reduce our exposure to the downside risk? When I coach entrepreneurs who are just starting their first business, I recommend that they continue with their day job until they can replace their income from the new venture. This provides the psychological safety and financial safety they need to continue with the risk of starting their business.

Who is your dream for?

Many people have a story that they tell themselves that prevents them from starting a big project, or that prevents them from even thinking about it in the first place. I'm too old, I'm too young, I'm not good with computers, I have kids, etc. You are making this too much about yourself. But when you are aligned with serving other people, when your mission is greater than you are, you are compelled. But let's say your mission is so big it becomes vague: 'I want to help empower female entrepreneurs!' But you don't actually know any women entrepreneurs who need empowering. Get in touch with a local organization for female entrepreneurs, ask questions, and figure out how to help one of them. And then when you go back and build your product/service/plan to empower more entrepreneurs, you can keep coming back to your image of just one person. Now you have made your efforts concrete – what would benefit this person? Sometimes podcast listeners ask me to cover a specific topic on the podcast. Then, when I do the interview, I can ask questions that will directly benefit one single audience member.

Getting more from your dreams

The cool thing about reality is that we often get more than our big dreams. Maybe your dream is for a video to go viral and get 1 million views. You can simply say 'my dream is for a video to get *at least* 1 million views. Even if we dream as big as we possibly can, there are an infinite number of possibilities, and we can't think of them all. So it's likely that you will get even more than you dream.

On the flip side, what if you try to go really big and fail? What if you want to hit the *New York Times* bestseller list, and you do a huge book tour, and lots of marketing but you don't hit the list and only sell 3,000 copies of your book? That's still pretty damn good, and probably way better than if you had said, 'I'll just put it out there and hope people like it.' You might sell 500 copies to people in your city and your Facebook friends.

Help other people dream big

Great leaders like Martin Luther King had a big dream for the future and they painted the picture for the rest of us to follow. As a coach, it is my job to see a bigger future for people than they can see for themselves. Your job is to create a compelling vision and enrol people in that vision.

Think about the most influential people in your life. These might be your parents, teachers, coaches, or someone that believed in you and saw a vision for your success. With their belief in you, they challenged you to step up to a better version of yourself. You can do this for other people by sharing what you see for them.

If you are interviewing for a position in an organization, do your homework and understand the true needs that they are trying to fill. You can do this by having conversations with people that work there already. Use your networking skills to make connections within the organization. If you can't find people in your exact target company, find people who have experience in the industry that can give you the lie of the land and tell you what some of the biggest challenges in that space are. This allows you to go into the interview with a plan, prepared for the challenges you expect to face. In a year's time, what will you accomplish in this organization? Help your employer see the bigger picture for your role. When you show up for the interview, break out your proposal for everything you want to accomplish in the six months to a year of your time there. This will also lead to more responsibility, autonomy, recognition and compensation.

Highlight the bright spots

Sometimes we need to see what is possible to open up our thinking. Focus your attention on the big ideas that are working well, what entrepreneur Aaron Hurst calls the bright spots. Hurst is the founder of the Taproot foundation where he created a $15 billion/year marketplace for pro bono work – a place where professionals who wanted to donate their expertise could be matched with the organizations that needed it. His goal was to change people's understanding of what was possible. But his major hurdle was that non-profits are not set up to manage the pro bono work they receive.

Aaron told me that he likes to think about creating 'fat start-ups' – a play on the Silicon Valley trend of lean start-ups. His goal is to create an entire marketplace rather than a monopoly, to enable a much broader impact. To help non-profits take advantage of the increased supply in pro bono work, Hurst had to show how the top performing non-profits structured their organization to take advantage of the pro bono resource. Knowing that he wanted to shift the entire market, he knew he needed to pull the right lever. Now at Imperative, Hurst's mission is to 'make all work feel like pro bono work'.

What social level are your dreams?

Aaron Hurst told me that there are three different social levels of how we like to impact change – at a personal, organizational, or societal level. So within medicine for example, you could be a doctor, a hospital administrator, or a public health policy maker respectively. It takes the self-awareness of how you want to make a difference in order to set for a big dream that aligns with your purpose. Knowing which level you want to impact change helps you avoid projects that don't suit you.

Big dreams in action

Love him or hate him, Elon Musk is a poster boy for dreaming big. He brings seemingly endless energy to his dream of making humanity a multi-planetary species. If you believe, like Musk, that our survival as a species depends on colonizing Mars (Musk, 2007), that immediately trivializes problems like 'we don't know how to do that', because obviously it has never been done before. Musk pushes himself and his companies to get results, even going as far as to risk his entire personal fortune and give up sleep for weeks at a time. For him, the stakes (humanity going extinct or not) are high enough to surmount all barriers. What are your stakes?

My friend and adventurer Dave Cornthwaite was just a normal 25 year old who went to work, played videogames and owned a cat. Until one day, he got a skateboard and realized that there could be way more to life. His first big skateboarding trip was across the continent of Australia, breaking the world record for distance skateboarded.

Dave then created Expedition 1000 – the quest to complete 25 journeys of 1,000 miles or more, each using a different mode of non-motorized transportation. He has completed 13 of the 25, and the trips include stand-up paddle boarding the length of the Mississippi River, swimming the Missouri River, and scootering across Japan. He has since founded a festival called Yestival, to help other people with their big adventure dreams. Dave said that, 'If I don't believe in myself, then nobody else will.'

Sean Conway is another adventurer who wanted to set the world record for being the fastest to cycle around the earth. However, a few weeks into his effort, he was hit by a car and had to pull the plug on the challenge. When I interviewed him on the Art of Adventure, Sean told me about how he was trying to set the cycling speed record for fastest to bike cross Europe, but a knee injury stopped him again. Despite these two glaring failures, the most important thing for Sean and you is to begin. Sean didn't know that he would succeed when he set out to become the first person to swim the length of Great Britain or complete the world's longest triathlon, but he was successful in both of those endeavours.

Should you share your dreams?

Each year I share my annual goals, themes and projects in a blog post, with the idea that it provides some accountability to achieving these goals. However, there is some evidence that suggests that we should not share our dreams right away with people (before we begin taking action on them), because simply sharing our dreams gives us the cognitive satisfaction from public acknowledgement.

Additionally, one of two things often happens: people who love you will support you no matter what and tell you that you will be successful. They may have no accurate perception of your career choices, but are behind you no matter what. This is great for confidence, but not for any realistic or helpful advice. The other thing that often happens when you share your dreams is that people will try to prevent you from starting. They say, 'that will never work, or you will lose your friends, or you will go bankrupt and become homeless, etc.' While these people might love you and care about your success, their own fear of what they don't know causes them to inaccurately assess your chances of achieving your dream.

Sometimes, we say that we don't have a big dream, when deep down we really do. How many times have we heard of someone who didn't get a promotion/picked for a team/make a sale etc and they came back and said 'I didn't really want that anyway'.

Own your awesome

In Australia they call it tall poppy syndrome – don't stand out above the crowd! In America we ridicule people who talk about the great parts of themselves – we call them braggarts or cocky. You probably don't even let yourself see the great things about you for fear that you will not be accepted.

We all want to be accepted and fit in, and so we dim our light in the hopes that other people will find us more accessible and easy to like. People even use complaining as small talk or a means of making connection with others. The subtle message this sends is 'let's all be NOT GREAT together'.

Among my coaching clients we make sure to start every call with a brag or a win or a celebration, because often this is the only place where people can really take in the good of what they have done or acknowledge a great part of themselves that they are letting shine.

At first, people find this to be challenging – to find something they have done well and own it. And then it becomes a huge relief, to finally start to accept the awesomeness in ourselves. Most people find it easier to see the greatness in others than they do in themselves. But how are you supposed to do great things in the world if you don't even acknowledge or let yourself show your best qualities?

What if we flipped the whole situation around? What if we encouraged people to truly accept that they are already awesome? What if instead of being afraid to be excited about the cool things you have done, you knew that it would bring you closer to people and be MORE loved and accepted? What do you want to OWN that you are brilliant at?

The 'What if?' game

At my AdventureQuest retreats, we play a game called 'What if?' What if I was the president of the world? What if I could fly? What if everyone agreed to help me? What if we ended world hunger? When you start asking big questions, you start coming up with big answers.

Use questions to guide your thoughts in the right direction.

EXERCISE – I have a dream

Write your own personal manifesto in the style of Martin Luther King Jr.'s 'I have a dream speech'. What are the things that you would like to see changed in the world? Who would you like to help? What gets you fired up? What cause would you camp out in the rain for? What is your vision for humanity? How can that be allied to a fulfilling new career?

Questions to expand your vision:

- What if you were to multiply by 10 the scope of your next activity – what would that look like?

- What if I gave you a million dollars to implement your next plan, how would that change your process?

- If you knew you would not fail, what would you do?

- If you felt 100 per cent worthy of any success that came your way, what would you do differently this year?

- What is something that you think is not possible now but might be possible in 10–20 years?

- If you could change or add anything to the world, what would you wish for the world to have?

Conclusion

We have talked about how to come up with a big dream and start planning for it, so that you can begin making progress even if you don't see all the steps. We have learned about the power of conviction in our dreams so that we don't sabotage our efforts. We learned why being a little crazy is actually a good thing, so that we can really make a difference. We learned how to plan for the worst-case scenario so that we are not left with any unknown fear. We highlighted some bright spots – big dreams that led to some amazing accomplishments, so that we can prove to ourselves that big goals can happen. And we learned how to focus on the great things we accomplish so that we avoid the trap of naysayers.

Works cited

Hamilton, R (nd) *Wealth Dynamics*. Retrieved 18 February 2018, from Wealth Dynamics: www.wealthdynamics.com/

Hewitt, A (2013, 4 November) *GameChangers: The world's top purpose-driven organizations*. Retrieved 5 March 2018, from Forbes: www.forbes.com/sites/skollworldforum/2013/11/04/gamechangers-the-worlds-top-purpose-driven-organizations/#5f90457077b6

Hill, N (1937) *Think and Grow Rich*, Dauphin Publications Inc

Logan, D C (2009, 1 March) *Known knowns, known unknowns, unknown unknowns and the propagation of scientific enquiry*. Retrieved 5 March 2018, from *Journal of Experimental Botany*: https://academic.oup.com/jxb/article/60/3/712/453685

Musk, E (2007) *Wired Science* (B Unger, Interviewer)

10
Fun and games

When human beings create and share experiences designed to delight or amaze, they often end up transforming society in more dramatic ways than people focused on more utilitarian concerns.
JOHNSON, 2017

I was looking around the bay in Cabo San Lucas, Mexico, when I realized that pretty much everything I saw in front of me was because people like to have fun. Cabo was a sleepy fishing village until someone decided this random place at the end of the Baja peninsula, would make a great vacation spot.

What I saw around me were: billion dollar resorts, hoverboards using water jets in the ocean, jet skis zipping around, beach volleyball games, beach dance clubs, whale watching tours, stand up paddleboard tours, paragliders behind boats, and plenty of people drinking margaritas. This whole city is built simply for joy.

Then I thought about the underlying expertise that was needed to make this happen – you would need fabulous builders and architects to build these resorts and then sales people to sell the times shares. To make a hoverboard, you need a variety of types of engineering expertise. To safely get close to a family of humpback whales, you need marine biology and boat piloting expertise. These are the economic drivers of fun.

Realizing that entire cities are built around different ideas of fun (Las Vegas, Aspen, etc) I started to wonder about how fun and play might be some of the most important drivers of the global economy, innovation, and excellence in careers. Companies such as Zappos have built their entire reputation on playfulness (and being nice), or Disney.

Everywhere you look, massive industries are built around delight and fun: movies, video games, sports, travel, theme parks, concerts, you name it. We are wired for fun and wired to play. This chapter will be about how to use fun, delight, play and curiosity as drivers for your own career success. Fun can clear the way for people to hear a more serious message as the Cartoonist Walk Kelly showed with his strip Pogo Possum. Play can lead to trying things that eventually lead to important discoveries or increased market share as in the case with Richard Feynman and Walmart respectively.

We are also going to talk about gamification. By now you have probably heard of gamification – basically it means taking ideas from games and applying them to other non-game pursuits. Most gamification efforts are pretty basic – like the Boy Scout merit badge system, there are badges and leaderboards and points you can earn. We are going to go deeper – how we can apply a gameful mindset to our career and ourselves.

Why are we bothering to talk about games you ask? I thought this was a serious career-minded book? Games are powerful. When I was in graduate school, the biochemistry game 'Fold It' came out to solve protein-folding problems. Researchers had been trying to figure out how a specific AIDS-related protein folded for decades, and after the game was released, players solved the problem in just three weeks (Peckham, 2011). *The Guardian* newspaper in the UK created a game with a crowdsourcing experiment where readers could sift through thousands of MP's expense reports in order to uncover potentially interesting stories.

Companies and organizations are using gamification to frame their challenges so that employees want to pitch in. This is a major part of talent acquisition and retention strategy that one of my previous interviewees on the podcast, Erica Dhawan, uses with her consulting firm Cotential. She teaches companies to use Shark Tank or Olympics style competitions so employees can participate in major initiatives within a company, even if they are already part of the executive decision-making team. In 2007, the World Food Programme launched a popular online game, Freerice, that it uses to attract advertising money to feed the hungry; more than three million pounds of rice have been donated so far (Heller, 2015).

When I created AdventureQuest trips, I had already been organizing ski trips for my college buddies for many years. In AdventureQuest, I use fun physical challenges like rock climbing and surfing to bring people together through shared challenge. I learned that the shared participation in fun activities increases the connectedness of our group. In the case of our ski trips, we were building on old friendships, and with AdventureQuest, shared challenges quickly bring strangers together as a tribe. When Nik Wood and I founded the weekly men's Ultimate Frisbee game in Ubud, Bali, our goal was to build shared community among men.

When I was running the Publishizer crowdfunding campaign to launch *Superconductors*, we used several game techniques. First, we offered rewards for different levels of support for the book. You could win things like a free coaching session with me or a talk at your organization. Both the book supporters and I were working on a time constraint – we were racing against the clock to get enough support that it would get the attention of a traditional publisher – and now that you are reading this book, you know that we succeeded! I also made sure to do a big push for support for the first day of the campaign, so that we would be at least 25 per cent of the way to our goal at the beginning. This is because people are much more likely to want to participate in a winning cause, and it establishes social proof right away. As I invited people to support the book project, I mentioned how many others had supported the project already and that we would all be working together to get this information out to more people that it could benefit. This makes us all become allies in the quest to publish a book.

Games can be customer-facing, employee-facing, and personal. Games can build customer engagement and help you acquire clients. Games can motivate and unify employees. Gamification gives you a powerful framework to be more engaged in your work and enhance your skills. This mindset allows you to take more risks and think outside the box. A game mindset allows you to set parameters around your goals and celebrate your successes along the way. Target has used games for its cashiers – a little red or green light flashes and tells them whether they have scanned an item in an optimal time (Hein, 2013). Games give us a clear way to win – there are no rules for a successful career other than the ones you set. Gamers are in control of the game they are playing. Some companies, such as Valve, are giving their employees control over the projects they work on, just like a freelancer would (Jenkins, 2017). We will use games to envision what a win looks like for our own career and life.

The value of delight

In his book *Wonderland*, Stephen Johnson shows how delight has been a driver of economies for millennia. Some of the earliest tools were in fact, musical instruments carved out of bone. Why were our ancestors making music instead of using their limited resources to produce more food or build houses for shelter? Perhaps because delight is such a strong driving force for humans that they were compelled to fiddle with music. And in the ancient Mediterranean, an ounce of purple dye from the Phoenician city of Tyre was worth more than an ounce of gold. Tyrolean purple was one of the most vivid and distinct dyes available, which all came back to the goal of us wearing clothes that we enjoyed looking great in. Delight has driven the global economy for millennia.

We humans are willing to invest a great deal of time and energy in perfecting our ability to have fun. As a cyclist, I have seen the development of bicycles over the last few decades incorporate composite technology, nano tech, ceramics, aerodynamic wind tunnel testing, and computer modelling. All this is to enhance the speed, comfort and durability of a bicycle, a toy with the primary objective of having us go wheeeee! Back in the beginning days of the Tour de France, it was illegal to use anything besides wooden wheels! Look how far we have come.

It amazes me that we are still inventing new sports! Think about wingsuit flying or kite boarding – these were not sports that existed until recently. In business and in career, there is the serious way to do things: solve a problem, fill a need, and then there is the fun way to do things: amaze, inspire and delight people. Of course you can do both at the same time.

Excitement pulls you forward

We have talked before about the need to have a strong WHY that keeps you going when you face challenges in your career. Of course, your why can include a strong component of 'because I love this' and delight. I am motivated to interview new people on the Art of Adventure because I get such pleasure from meeting new amazing people and learning from them. I also love working with my coaching clients. And, according to *INC* magazine, engaged teams grow profits three times faster than disengaged ones (Jenkins, 2017).

It is much better to have an innate interest in your work and feel pulled towards it rather than feeling an obligation to do it because you have to. We all need something to look forward to. Interest goes hand in hand with curiosity – get curious about what you can create in your career. What is possible for you? Some of the great discoveries and inventions are often simply scientists following their curiosity and messing around – take Richard Feynman's Nobel Prize-winning work in physics, which came from him spinning plates around in the Cornell University cafeteria (Blinder, nd).

Play as part of our humanness

One of the most common complaints I hear from the corporate world is that people feel like it is not fun. One of my clients told me that attending a regular meeting felt like they were 'walking on eggshells', and could not express joy or speak their mind for fear of upsetting one of the delicate personalities in the room.

What if we created a world where business and productive workplaces were fun?

In nearly all mammals, play is a chance for young animals to learn and push their limits. Think of puppies or kittens play fighting and rolling around or a deer bounding through the wood this way and that. We have already learned in this book that we receive a surge of dopamine – a happiness inducing neurotransmitter when we solve a problem or use our creativity. We can use our biology to hack our happiness by structuring our lives and our career to consistently encounter interesting challenges.

Play in science and innovation

We know that Thomas Edison was a tinkerer and played with thousands of different filaments before he found the right carbonized filament of plant matter that he used in his invention of the incandescent light bulb (Institute, 2018). In its essence, tinkering and play can be a purposeful yet fun way to create new things for the world. For many years, Google utilized a philosophy called 20 per cent time, which let employees work on personal projects they believed could benefit the company. This led to some of Google's most well-known offerings such as Gmail, Google Maps and Adsense (D'Onfro, 2015).

Playing around was a major driver of the beginning of inquiry in our virology lab when I was in grad school. What is often not understood outside the laboratory is that before we design the full, official experiment that leads to a publication with some new finding, we are doing lots of 'off the cuff' experiments.

What this looked like in our lab was that I would go to Yellowstone National Park, trek out across a plain full of hot springs and take samples along the way from the ones that I knew were especially hot or acidic. Then back in the lab I would try to grow whatever was in the hot spring by adding a small sample to a variety of different nutrient rich broths to see if anything would grow.

Only after I finally was able to establish a growing culture of an extremophile microbe, was I ready to start the official experiment to study and determine the species of the microbes and viruses in the hot springs. The same thing happens in business – we create a product and then do a beta launch to a small number of people to make sure there is a good product or market fit, before we release the final version to the whole world. Even then, offerings are constantly evolving. Lets see what happens if we add an XYZ feature.

In your career you can run little experiments. You can leave to work at a rival company and if it doesn't work, come back to your old job. Or you can try a side gig and realize that you prefer that and go full time. The important thing when playing around with your career is that you have clarity about what the experiment is telling you. How will you know if a change you make is actually better or teaches you something or points you in a different direction? This is why it is so important to have a weekly clarity session with yourself or a coach.

In this clarity session you want to be asking yourself things like: Do I feel my work on this project is meaningful? Who do I need to show up as to excel at my goal in the next week? What was I surprised by when I took on this new challenge? What did I learn about the type of work I value? What were the types of things that felt easy for me? By taking a moment to see if you are getting colder or warmer in relation to your ideal career, you avoid getting locked into a path without perspective.

Strategic play

During the most recent AdventureQuest retreat in the Ozark Mountains of Arkansas, our group went rock climbing. We spent the whole day coming up with analogies for how rock climbing is like running a business:

- There are no rules.
- What happens in your mind when you fail or fall?
- Receiving encouragement helps.
- Having a safety net allows you to take risks.
- You can move laterally around a problem.
- There are infinite ways up the rock and different people utilize different techniques to get to the top.
- The 5.5 rated route felt too easy by the end of the day as we had worked our way up to climbing 5.9 (climbing difficulty ratings go from 5.0 to 5.15).

People reported that after the trip they approached problems at work in an entirely different light. They were thinking more playfully and it allowed them to come up with completely new solutions to problems.

Fun created Walmart

In America, one of the great stories in business is that of the self-made billionaire, Sam Walton, the founder of Walmart. In his book, *Made in America*, Walton tells numerous stories of the competitive advantage Walmart gained through play. Walmart was one of the first stores to play around with big audacious displays outside the store. Once they made a giant pyramid of laundry detergent boxes simply as an interesting sculpture to draw people into the store. The Walmart corporate Saturday morning meetings or shareholder meetings are punctuated with dancing and music in between the business.

The happiness of pursuit

The idea of a quest is as old as the quest for the Holy Grail. I run into more and more people who are working their way through a bucket list. A quest is simply a larger framework for achieving something. Often the nature of a quest is something that calls to you, as in the call to adventure in the Heroes Journey cycle. Here are some of my favourite quests that guests of the Art of Adventure have set for themselves.

For American writer, Chris Guillebeau, who I interviewed on the podcast, his quest was to visit every country in the world before his 35th birthday. For explorer Dave Cornthwaite, his quest is to complete 25 journeys of 1,000 miles or more, each with a different mode of non-motorized transportation. For British artist Anne-Laure Carruth, her quest was to circumnavigate the Mediterranean in a Land Rover and do artistic collaborations in each country. Two examples of my own quests are to record 300 podcast episodes (200 down, 100 to go), and live three months or more on each of the six inhabited continents (four down, two to go).

Quests are a much more long-term goal than daily tasks or challenges. You can pick a quest directly or tangentially in service of your career. For example, my quest for 300 podcast interviews directly impacts my career as an interviewer, whereas living on all the continents exposes me to many business ideas and styles that might benefit my career. Having these long-term goals within your career can lead to greater happiness and fulfilment as well. Because you have declared a clear framework for a quest, you will be able to quickly seize opportunities in service of your objective, and ignore inappropriate ones.

Like any goal, you need to have clear measurable criteria for your quest. This also means setting a deadline for completion. You could even consider working your way through all the skill acquisition in this book as a type of quest if you put some parameters around it.

The joy in a quest is that generally your goal is something big, audacious and risky. Don't let the risk or the perception of risk hold you back! Because these quests are significant, know that they will take, time, focus and energy. By choosing to undertake a quest, you are closing the door on other opportunities. You can't complete a year's or decade's long quest without persistence. In your career or as an entrepreneur, simply showing up over and over again will smooth over many of the pitfalls along the way.

When you are starting your quest, give yourself permission to daydream and fully envision the result of what might happen. Daydreaming allows you to think bigger than you would otherwise – you have to let yourself go there.

As with the outcome of the heroes' journey, you as an adventurer, someone who undertakes a quest will come back with the treasure. This means you will be changed forever and increasingly more valuable to your tribe. You will have gained skills, confidence, resilience and perseverance that you will be able to bring to the your career and your community. These career quests are so much fun they can be addictive – just make sure you give yourself time to settle in and take advantage of your new situation and experience.

Gamification

In his TEDx Talk, gamification expert Yu-kai Chou introduces his audience to how we can access the game elements and add them to our daily lives to make boring things more exciting. Chou reminds us that the human brain has a much better time with instant gratification than long-term goals. Gamification can highlight the small wins along the way to a larger objective, which is what the Nike + app does by showing users daily feedback on how close users are to their daily goals, which fuel our needs of accomplishment and empowerment. People using the app can also challenge friends, which brings in the element of social relatedness. A long-running game from airlines and credit cards involves earning airline miles, elite status levels, and ways of redeeming your miles and points. This would tick the accomplishment, and ownership boxes (Chou, 2017).

I attended marketing consultant John Abbott's talk at Freedom X Fest, and learned that online contests are gamified ways to bulk up your customer base. The contests go viral by letting people enter a contest multiple times if they share or tag their friends. Food bloggers may use a giveaway of a blender – something that their audience loves – in order to build their tribe of followers. A contest is generally well aligned with the algorithm that social media networks are using. You may be able to gain more entries into the contest (and a greater chance of winning) if you tag your friends and they also follow the contest holder. Contest entries can be a great way to learn about your customers and their behaviour in relation to your offering. If you are able to get your prizes donated by various partners, you can leverage their existing networks as well. It doesn't really matter what platform your audience prefers – I've seen contests run across various social media platforms with a central contest webpage that collects the entries. So keep Yu-kai Chou's core drivers in mind, and always be on the lookout for ways that games help you connect with and grow your customer base (Ledgard, 2017).

GAMIFICATION CASE STUDY: THE GREAT E-COURSE ADVENTURE

I interviewed online educator Bradley Morris about his video training course – the Great E-Course adventure (GEA). This was the first online training I had seen that blended the ideas of your standard video-based lecture course with something like a video game story. The GEA creators knew that one of the major problems with the online course industry is that only a small percentage of people actually finish their training (Seth Godin stated on the Tim Ferriss show that most courses have a 97 per cent drop-off rate and his own courses had more than 80 per cent drop-off rate). They knew their material was good, but if they could also crack the code to enable their students to go all the way through the process, that would make their own training so much more valuable and would ensure a profitable online course.

Their strategy is based on the analogy of how creating your first e-course is like climbing a mountain. The creators, Bradley Morris and Andy Feist use different elements of gamification to make their course more compelling. They have a merit badge system similar to what the boy scouts use. When you move from one lesson to the next, you earn badges. But you can also earn money called 'Bajillion', that you can spend on real-life things that are useful for course creators – things like lighting systems or software for editing video.

Each new module in the course is a new location on the mountains. There are places like 'Validation Swamps' and 'Automatora river'. There are magical beings that serve as mentors and guides in these locations. Even the videos themselves are done with greenscreen and overlaid with the backdrop of their location on the mountain.

Which course would you rather take – one where you watch a series of videos, or one where you yourself are the hero of a journey that leads to the outcome you desire (in this case, making money from teaching what you know through an e-course)?

The importance of healthy competition

I ran on the cross-country and track and field teams in college as a distance runner. Each week during the season, results from meets around the country would come in and we would compare our times with those of our rivals. And each day we would head out for workouts and some runners would run a half step ahead of others, which would cause the pace to creep up faster and faster. Now, with the Strava exercise app, cyclists and runners can compare their GPS measured times against others over the same segment of road or trail. The first time I used the app, I experienced the joy of briefly holding one of the fastest times on a segment – until someone faster came along! I tried a few more times to beat the new best time – focus efforts I otherwise might not have made.

Many of us have a natural joy in competing and comparing ourselves to others. While this might not be good for your ego when you look on Facebook and compare yourself to everyone else who is supposedly leading the most amazing life, it does spur you to be your best when you can compare on a standardized metric. For example, sales organizations incentivize people to reach the highest number of sales in a quarter with prizes or financial incentives going to the winner.

Crowdsourced innovation

In 2009, I was unemployed in the great recession, and I was testing out various online money-making schemes. I tried being a secret shopper and a product reviewer, and I also joined Napkin Labs, which was a crowdsourced innovation platform. Companies would hire Napkin Labs to create new product for them, and in turn Napkin Labs would bring together a diverse group of 25–50 people from different fields to help solve the problem and create a new product. I knew that the innovators over at IDEO were doing something similar and I wanted to see how it worked in practice.

At the end of the project, usually three weeks, you would be compensated financially for the scope of your contribution. You would earn more if you contributed more ideas, and if other members of the team liked your idea and up-voted it. Even if you had a controversial idea, you would earn points for the discussion you generated. There were bonuses that went to people whose ideas were eventually implemented by the originators of the problem. In this system we were not only trying to solve the main puzzle of creating a new hammock, shopping cart, etc, but we were also playing a game where we were instantly rewarded for our contribution and could compare ourselves to the other people in the team.

I remember going all in on one project to see if I could sit at the top of the leaderboard. I guess there were a couple of other unemployed people working on this project at the same time because every time

I logged on to the community space, someone would have surpassed my points total and I would have to generate a lot more ideas to regain my place at the top of the points total. Without me even seeing the bigger picture of the game elements, I was pouring my best ideas into this project and the customer was getting exactly what they needed, without having to force or cajole me into my efforts. We want to use game structure to get the best work from people.

A framework for thinking

I've always loved board games, because it gives you a clear goal – win the game – and clear rules for how to do that. Often within those rules however, you can use any means possible to accomplish your goal. Some of my favourite games are Settlers of Catan, Risk and Monopoly, which involve a component of trade or negotiation, alliances and cooperation. Which means that I am going to try every psychological technique in the book, from coercion to persuasion to reciprocity to social proof in order to create conditions to allow me to win the game. Games expand our creativity by forcing us to win in a specific way. We already learned in Chapter 3 that it expands our creative thinking when we can narrow our focus. In your everyday career life, when you clearly define how to win, you will come up with better strategies to do so.

During a game, we are often willing to take bigger risks and try new things, because the real consequences are only losing the game (but I still hate losing). The difference between the times when we are playing games and real life, is that in real life we often play it much safer than we do in games, thereby robbing ourselves of a chance for victory. Because real money, health and relationships are on the line, we play much smaller and more conservatively. But what if I told you that many of the perceived negative consequences for taking risks like you do in games are not real? They are part of our natural wiring to focus on threats, whereas the potential upside for taking calculated risks is that we win big. So what if we approached our careers like we do our favourite games? Would you be more willing to take a chance and roll the dice?

Games are useful because they narrow our number of competitors. We aren't trying to beat the entire world, we are only trying to beat our immediate competitors. It's nearly impossible to try to compare yourself against the entire world (which happens on massive freelance sites like upwork or fiverr), but much easier when you have an internal competition going with the other people on your sales team.

Video game designer Jane McGonigal is one of the premier game theorists on how game thinking benefits our lives and careers. She argues that we can use games for post-traumatic growth – where people turn a big catastrophe into a greater appreciation and zest for life. It's the way we view and respond to our stress that leads us to growth. What if you never had to go through a traumatic event in the first place? This is what McGonigal calls post-ecstatic growth. This is the type of growth that occurs after finishing a marathon, stopping smoking, or writing a novel (McGonigal, 2015).

Gamification as a personal tool

Remember your short introduction to the 'heroes journey' in the storytelling chapter? Video games often use the development of the hero to move the story of the game along. There are ways to level up, fight bigger and bigger battles, get new tools, acquire new skills, etc. Games can be addictive because this reality is so compelling as a story for us.

What if you were to view your own life through the lens of a game? What if you make yourself the hero of your own story? This is exactly what Jane McGonigal did for herself when she was healing from a traumatic brain injury, and what she has created for others with the SuperBetter game framework.

Here are the rules of SuperBetter and how to apply the game to your career:

1 *Create a challenge for yourself.* Examples of good challenges: beating depression, overcoming anxiety, coping with chronic illness or pain, finding a new job, adopting a new habit, developing a talent, improving a skill.

2 *Collect and activate power-ups.* Power-up examples: get some sunshine, do a dance break, eat something good, listen to your favourite music.

3 *Battle bad guys.* These are the things that stand in your way of completing your challenge. If you are looking for a new job, bad guys might include nerves before an interview, doubt over your qualifications, or not following up with opportunities.

4 *Go on quests.* These are smaller challenges to help you with your big challenge. Daily quests help you, the hero, build skills, strength and abilities. Make these small enough that you can complete in a day (small wins) so that you build up your 'I can do this!' feeling.

5 *Recruit allies.* Ask other people to join you in your game – they can be a source of advice and support or suggest new quests and power-ups. You might want to choose someone else who is working on their career or similar challenge at the same time.

6 *Adopt a secret identity.* This helps you frame the way you approach your challenge, and also distance yourself from a problem, which helps keep your eye on the big picture. See the exercise on creating your superhero identity for help with this.

7 *Go for epic wins.* This is where you think bigger for yourself (see Chapter 10) and take on a challenge that leads you to a complete levelling up. These challenges should be outside your comfort zone and at the limit of your abilities. Career examples: connect with a potential client/employer/partner every day for a month, or reach out to an influencer in your field and be a guest on their blog/podcast/YouTube channel.

EXERCISE – Design your game

Using the SuperBetter framework, create a career-focused challenge for yourself. It could be getting a new job, mastering one of the skills in this book, implementing a habit to boost your career performance, or pick your own.

Your life as a sport

My friend Nik Wood, founder of Life Athletics, asks the question, 'How can we treat life like a game or a sport?' Since we have already looked at McGonigal's game framework, let's see how we can use a sports analogy as well. When Nik and I were housemates in Bali, we would often have a pow wow at the front door before leaving for the day. Nik would ask, 'How will you know if you win the day today?' Basically this means, you get to set your own bar for achievement and then rise to meet the challenge you issue for yourself. Sometimes this means showing up in a certain way – 'I'm going to be a vocal leader today' or hitting measurable goals 'I'm going to talk to five new people at the party'.

✓ Nik started to view every area of life as trainable after he started asking himself 'what areas in my life am I out of shape in?' Nik told me that training in one area of life is often applicable to another area of life. For example: when I was a recent college graduate, I was advised to put my athletic training on my résumé and talk about it during interviews. Now that I am hiring people and building teams I automatically assume that people who have met huge athletic challenges will be able to transfer that perseverance and skill acquisition to a business setting.

CASE STUDY: I BEAT MY GIRLFRIEND IN A GAME WE MADE UP

My partner Heidi and I made up a game last year. We decided that we wanted to have more fun and we wanted to incentivize ourselves to do more of certain activities. At the end of each day we tallied up points. Ways to earn points include listening to a podcast, reading a book, earning money, completing a workout, doing something brave or spending quality time with friends.

There is both a stick and carrot incorporated into our game: the winner gets a massage from the loser – or the loser has to pay for a professional massage for the winner. We found that earning points each day was an exciting reward for focusing our efforts on important things. We also enjoyed keeping streaks alive – at one time, Heidi had earned a point for 15 days in a row.

If you are working on creating a certain habit in your life, if you spend an entire month playing a game where you earn points for an activity, you will have worked it into your normal schedule by the end of the month. Within my own team, we have a contest going to see who can refer the most new clients. The rewards are progressive; with each new customer referral, they unlock a new level of rewards.

GAME FRAMEWORK CASE STUDY: START-UP WEEKEND

In Ubud, Bali, the local co-working space Hubud holds start-up weekends a couple of times a year. In just 54 hours over a weekend, people get together for a start-up competition. This isn't just a group getting together for talk business, it's a contest to see who can create the most complete business concept in a weekend. At the end of the weekend all the projects are judged, and the winner gets mentorship, funding and opportunities to grow their brand new business.

I saw first-hand how people participating went all-in on their idea and effort. Some people that participate already have an idea for a start-up, others are going to find partners or mentors. Because we have time constraints and a format constraint, people are competing to win the weekend by presenting their work in front of a panel of judges. You may end the weekend with a business that is fully ready to go, along with investors and mentors.

The progression of a start-up weekend is beginning with pitching your idea and forming or joining a team. Once your team has formed around an idea, the second day is full of finding customers, building the product, doing market research, getting coaching, and refining the business model. Just like in Chapter 3, we know that time and format constraints help you be more creative. I love this model because just like with other goals, there is a clear end point – the end of the 54 hours, and a clear way to win the competition – be voted first by the experienced judges.

Many people have a tendency to procrastinate taking action by reading one more blog post or book, which is great for your initial immersion, but only action can lead to results. For many, the confines of this game called 'Startup Weekend' is the first time that they have actually tried running a business. So while it feels like a game, the business created there are real, working businesses. Outside of this experience, an individual might be paralysed by analysing their options for years. Because of the game structure of start-up weekends, it takes the pressure off and makes starting a business fun and lets people take big risks.

Play and flow

My friend Jiro Taylor is an executive coach and he leads flow state retreats for his clients all over the world. They do things like surfing and skiing, so they can learn to inhabit the flow state, which they then use later on the job.

I used to work in a microbiology laboratory, where we would do hundreds of tests everyday on different food products to ensure they were not contaminated. It took me a few weeks to learn all the protocols and procedures for these tests. Once I understood the process, I had nothing left to learn and found myself getting bored. So I came up with a game: I would time myself on a series of test – trying to figure out how I could batch different steps, and run multiple tests at the same time. I thought of it as a way to improve my assembly line of test results. I would try doing one test at a time through to completion and compare that to doing one step at a time for 25 tests and then moving on to the next step for all 25. I played around with my workstation so that I would have to physically move the least amount, this making everything more efficient. I played around with teaming up with another microbiologist to see if we could get more than twice the work done together than either of us could get done on our own. In the end, we probably improved our speed by 25–50 per cent, which of course improved our bottom line, but the most important part was that by playing this speed game, we were continually introducing new challenges for ourselves. Without this type of challenge, our skills would have quickly surpassed the work, and we would have been supremely bored. If you ever find yourself in this situation, the first thing I would suggest is to look at where you can expand your career possibilities. Barring an increase in responsibility or new interesting tasks, your best bet is to have fun doing the thing you are doing.

You can apply this same speed contest with yourself each time you are doing a chore. When I used to mow lawns as a teenager, I was in business with another athlete who went on to set a world record in speed skating. We would time ourselves to see how fast we could run back and forth and mow the lawn more quickly each time. Once you hit the limit of your physical exertion, your only choice is to innovate with better, more efficient mowing patterns.

Conclusion

What a fun chapter! You learned about how delight is a powerful driver of our economy. You learned how play can lead to unexpected discoveries in science and marketing (Feynman and Walmart). You learned how companies are using games to grow their customer base and retain employees. You learned several frameworks of thinking to advance your career: the SuperBetter game, quests, and thinking of life as a sport. You saw some case studies of different personal and group game experiences. And you learned how the right level of challenge can lead you to more personal enjoyment of your activities. Many of my clients benefit greatly from building more fun into their careers – which framework will you try first?

Works cited

Blinder, S M (nd) *Feynman's Wobbling Plate*. Retrieved 22 February 2018, from Wolfram Demonstrations Project: http://demonstrations.wolfram. com/FeynmansWobblingPlate/

Chou, Y-k (2017, 12 January) *Top 10 Marketing Gamification Cases You Won't Forget*. Retrieved 22 February 2018, from Yu-kai Chou: Gamification & Behavioral Design: http://yukaichou.com/ gamification-examples/top-10-marketing-gamification-cases-remember/

D'Onfro, J (2015, 17 April) *The truth about Google's famous '20% time' policy*. Retrieved 22 February 2018, from *Business Insider*: www.busi-nessinsider.com/google-20-percent-time-policy-2015-4/?IR=T

Hein, R (2013, 6 June) *How to Use Gamification to Engage Employees*. Retrieved 22 February 2018, from CIO: www.cio.com/article/2453330/ careers-staffing/how-to-use-gamification-to-engage-employees.html

Heller, N (2015, 14 September) *High Score: A new movement seeks to turn life's challenges into a game*. Retrieved 22 February 2018, from *The New Yorker*: www.newyorker.com/magazine/2015/09/14/high-score

Institute, F (2018) *Edison's Lightbulb*. Retrieved 4 March 2018, from Franklin Institute: www.fi.edu/history-resources/edisons-lightbulb

Jenkins, R (2017, 7 February) *7 Ways Gamification Can Help Retain and Engage Millennials*. Retrieved 22 February 2018, from INC: www.inc. com/ryan-jenkins/how-to-gamify-career-paths-to-retain-and-engage-millennials.html

Johnson, S (2017) *Wonderland: How play made the modern world,* Riverhead Books.

Ledgard, J (2017) *How to Create Contests that Boost Revenues – 7 KickoffLabs Customer Case Studies.* Retrieved 22 February 2018, from Kickoff Labs: https://kickofflabs.com/blog/create-contests-boost-revenues-7-kickofflabs-customer-case-studies/

McGonigal, J (2015) *SuperBetter: A revolutionary approach to getting stronger, happier, braver and more resilient – powered by the science of games,* Penguin

Peckham, M (2011, 19 September), *Foldit Gamers Solve AIDS Puzzle that Baffled Scientists for a Decade.* Retrieved 4 March 2018, from Time: http://techland.time.com/2011/09/19/foldit-gamers-solve-aids-puzzle-that-baffled-scientists-for-decade/

INDEX